Does Policy Analysis Matter?

THE AARON WILDAVSKY FORUM
FOR PUBLIC POLICY

Edited by Lee S. Friedman

This series is intended to sustain the intellectual excitement that Aaron Wildavsky created for scholars of public policy everywhere. The ideas in each volume are initially presented and discussed at a public lecture and forum held at the University of California.

Aaron Wildavsky, 1930–1993

"Your prolific pen has brought real politics to the study of budgeting, to the analysis of myriad public policies, and to the discovery of the values underlying the political cultures by which peoples live. You have improved every institution with which you have been associated, notably Berkeley's Graduate School of Public Policy, which as Founding Dean you quickened with your restless innovative energy. Advocate of freedom, mentor to policy analysts everywhere."

(Yale University, May 1993, from text granting the honorary degree of Doctor of Social Science)

Does Policy Analysis Matter?

*Exploring Its Effectiveness
in Theory and Practice*

Edited by

Lee S. Friedman

To Geno,

Best always,

Lee

UNIVERSITY OF CALIFORNIA PRESS

University of California Press, one of the most distinguished university presses in the United States, enriches
lives around the world by advancing scholarship in the
humanities, social sciences, and natural sciences. Its
activities are supported by the UC Press Foundation and
by philanthropic contributions from individuals and
institutions. For more information, visit www.ucpress.edu.

University of California Press
Oakland, California

Library of Congress Cataloging-in-Publication Data

Names: Friedman, Lee S., editor, contributor.
Title: Does policy analysis matter? : exploring its
    effectiveness in theory and practice / edited by
    Lee S. Friedman.
Description: Oakland, California : University of
    California Press, [2016] | Series: Wildavsky Forum
    Series, vol. 10 | Includes bibliographical references
    and index.
Identifiers: LCCN 2016039695 (print) | LCCN 2016042079
    (ebook) | ISBN 9780520287396 (cloth : alk. paper) |
    ISBN 9780520287402 (pbk. : alk. paper) |
    ISBN 9780520962538 (ebook)
Subjects: LCSH: Policy sciences—United States—
    Evaluation. | Political planning—United States. |
    United States—Government policy.
Classification: LCC H97 .D63 2016 (print) | LCC H97 (ebook) |
    DDC 361.6/10973—dc23
LC record available at https://lccn.loc.gov/2016039695

Manufactured in the United States of America

26 25 24 23 22 21 20 19 18 17
10 9 8 7 6 5 4 3 2 1

CONTENTS

CONTRIBUTORS

Lee S. Friedman, Professor of the Graduate School and Professor Emeritus of Public Policy, University of California, Berkeley.

John A. Hird, Dean of the College of Social and Behavioral Sciences and Professor of Political Science and Public Policy, University of Massachusetts Amherst.

Eric M. Patashnik, Director of Public Policy Program and Julis-Rabinowitz Professor of Public Policy, Watson Institute for International and Public Affairs and Department of Political Science, Brown University.

Justin Peck, Assistant Professor of Political Science, San Francisco State University.

M. Suzanne Donovan, Executive Director, Strategic Education Research Partnership, Washington, DC.

FIGURES AND TABLES

FIGURES

TABLES

PREFACE

This book had its origins at the 20th annual Aaron Wildavsky
Forum for Public Policy, held at the University of California,
Berkeley, on April 10, 2014. Aaron Wildavsky was the founding
dean of UC Berkeley's Goldman School of Public Policy, one of
the visionaries who saw the potential of creating the new profession of public policy analysis. Aaron loved intellectual engagement, and the Forum was created in his honor to foster engagement on important issues of public policy. It seemed fitting to
mark this special anniversary of the Forum by taking stock of
our knowledge about the effects of the profession that he helped
to create. The volume contributors began their work by agreeing to participate in the 20th anniversary Forum.

The question that lies at the center of this volume's inquiry is
just how well democratic decision making can incorporate
knowledge and expertise into its institutional framework through
the work of public policy analysts. There is the further question
of how the answer might vary with the specific decision-making
institution considered, as well as with the specific policy area

under consideration. While there may be few people who would aspire to uninformed decision making in any public area, there are also few people who would aspire to undemocratic decision making in that same public area. The key is the extent to which policy-analytic expertise can complement democratic decision making rather than substitute for it.

The questions that motivate this volume are of interest to all citizens. Thus the essays herein are useful not just to those interested in the work of the graduate public policy schools, but to anyone studying public policy making. Colleges and universities offer many courses to both undergraduate and graduate students that introduce them to how public policy is made, perhaps called "Making Public Policy" or "Introduction to Public Policy." The short table at the end of this preface suggests good choices for assigning specific chapters in this volume to accompany particular lecture topics in those courses.

We are grateful to all of the Forum participants, and particularly the discussants Sarah Anzia, John Ellwood, David Kirp, Amy Lerman, Jane Mauldon, and Jesse Rothstein, whose comments have helped to improve this book. We are also grateful to David Weimer, Joseph Cordes, and the anonymous reviewers of this manuscript for their careful reading and constructive suggestions that have led to substantial improvements in the final product. Finally, we are grateful to Cambridge University Press for its permission to include the work of Eric Patashnik and Justin Peck, which appears in a slightly earlier version in the volume, *Governing in a Polarized Age: Elections, Parties and Political Representation in America,* edited by Alan S. Gerber and Eric Schickler (Cambridge University Press, 2016).

All of the contributors to this volume value highly the intellectual excitement and engagement that Aaron Wildavsky brought to those around him and that the Forum in his honor continues to do through its Berkeley lectures and through the books in this series. Therefore, we have assigned any royalties that may accrue to this volume to the University of California's Aaron Wildavsky Forum for Public Policy, in full support of its worthy mission.

Lee S. Friedman

TABLE I

Suggested Chapter Links to Lecture Topics in Courses on
Making Public Policy

Chapters	Lecture Topics
Chapter 1: Policy Making and Policy Analysis	The Purpose of Public Policies Studying Public Policy
Chapter 2: How Effective Is Policy Analysis?	Values and Knowledge in Policy Making Bureaucracy Regulatory Policy
Chapter 3: Can Congress Do Policy Analysis?	The Legislative Process Institutions and Interest Groups Agenda Setting Making Policy Decisions
Chapter 4: Policy Analysis and Design for Complex Services	Policy Implementation Policy Design Education Policy
Chapter 5: Summary and Future Directions	Evaluating Public Policies Analyzing Public Policy

CHAPTER ONE

Public Policy Making and Public Policy Analysis

LEE S. FRIEDMAN

In all societies, there are reasons why the people want some collective actions. One common reason is to establish order through rules and regulations that define such things as property rights and criminal activity and enforcement mechanisms like civil courts and a criminal justice system. Societies undertake collective actions for the security of the group, to promote the public health (like a clean water supply), to promote commerce (roads and bridges, traffic controls), to provide education, to provide for the disadvantaged, and many other reasons. The choice of these collective actions, or public policies, is the essence of why we have governments. Governments vary greatly in terms of the institutional processes used to decide public policies and the specific public policies that they adopt.

But in all cases, governments face tough choices about how specifically to achieve their aims. Even those with substantial tax

I am grateful to those colleagues who kindly read and offered helpful comments on earlier drafts of this chapter: Dan Acland, Janet Flammang, Alex Gelber, John Hird, Eric Patashnik, Bob Reich, and Gene Smolensky.

bases and tax authority have limited resources that force difficult trade-offs. Just how much is available to spend on, say, education, depends on how efficiently the society uses its resources in providing other important things: security, clean water, transportation infrastructure, and attending to private needs (since raising taxes leaves taxpayers with less for their private needs). Thus it is generally in a society's interest to use its resources efficiently for all activities, although how to do this is no simple matter.

This book is about the effort to improve governmental policy making through the development, beginning in the 1950s, of a new profession composed of advisors and public managers trained in public policy analysis and strategic public management. The use of such professionals has become commonplace at all levels of government in the United States and in many other countries around the world. A central question that we examine is this: What have we learned about the effects of this new profession on public policies and on policy making? Does policy analysis matter? Closely related to this central question is another one: Does what we have learned offer lessons for whether and how policy analysis can be improved?

This chapter reviews briefly the development and growth of the policy-analytic profession. Then it offers some perspective on the research to date that has attempted to assess its effects, a perspective that emphasizes some important differences across the many types of governmental settings that utilize policy analysis, and the methodological difficulties that assessment efforts confront. Finally, it introduces the following essays, which provide more detailed examinations of the practice of policy analysis within particular governmental settings. The book's concluding chapter offers a summary and suggestions for future research.

THE DEVELOPMENT AND GROWTH OF
PUBLIC POLICY ANALYSIS AND
MANAGEMENT

Put simply, policy analysis is the science and art of using knowledge to assist policy makers so that better choices will be made. Historically, government decision makers have often called upon those with expertise to assist them in reaching their decisions. Architects and engineers, for example, are typically involved when deciding if a new bridge can or should be constructed, or how to make a new public building safe, functional, and aesthetic. But this book concerns a new professional class of advisors that began developing during the 1950s in the United States. This new profession assists policy makers in understanding better their alternatives and relevant considerations for choosing among them.

One of the earliest examples is the nonprofit RAND Corporation, a think tank that was formed in 1948 and hired operations researchers, economists, psychologists, and others "to further and promote scientific, educational, and charitable purposes, all for the public welfare and security of the United States of America." These researchers used their tools to develop "systems analysis" intended initially to help military decision makers understand better their alternatives and to make more informed choices from among them.[1] In the early 1960s, when Robert McNamara became secretary of defense under President John F. Kennedy, he ordered that this analytic approach be instituted for all military decision making in the form of "planning, programming and budgeting systems."

The policy-analytic method was also shown to be useful in considering alternative approaches to municipal services like police protection and to social services like health care. In 1965 a substantial broadening in the use of policy analysis took place. President Lyndon B. Johnson mandated its adoption throughout the federal government.

New offices of policy analysis, or policy planning, or policy evaluation were opened in most federal agencies. Some existing offices were reconstituted to provide the new services. For example, Congress wanted its own analytic advice on issues of its choosing. It already had the Legislative Reference Service, created in 1914 to assist congressional committees through librarian services that provided them with reliable factual information. In 1970 the Legislative Reorganization Act renamed it the Congressional Research Service and significantly expanded its responsibilities to include conducting its own nonpartisan policy analyses for Congress. In 1974 Congress also created the Congressional Budget Office (CBO) staffed with analysts to provide nonpartisan advice on budgetary policy matters. So both the executive and legislative branches of the federal government began to employ this new professional class of analysts to help make more informed policy choices.

Much new effort was devoted to cost-effectiveness analysis (comparing the cost of alternative programs designed to achieve the same end), benefit-cost analysis (comparing the value of a program's benefits to its costs), and other systematic comparisons to enable more informed policy choices. All of these analytic efforts put a new emphasis on considering the governmental outcomes achieved in relation to the cost of achieving them. These analyses drew primarily on economic and quantitative skills. Almost always there are alternative means to achieve the same ends, and policy analysis could contribute objective findings to allow more reasoned policy choices. The policy analysts in these offices did not have any power other than that of reason; if their nonpartisan work had influence, it was through the decision makers whom they were advising.

While this early use of professional nonpartisan analysts showed promise, its ability to achieve its intent was limited by the analysts' lack of training or expertise in other skills that matter greatly in federal decision making. These include political and legal skills, understanding bureaucratic processes, and communicating effectively in the policy-making environment. Furthermore, how well policies work depends not just on their design but also on how well they are managed when implemented. In an attempt to address these weaknesses, new types of graduate schools were formed in the late 1960s and 1970s by the country's leading universities: Berkeley, Harvard, Princeton, Duke, Texas, Carnegie Mellon, Michigan, and others. They created new interdisciplinary Public Policy graduate schools to train professionals in public policy analysis and strategic management. These professionals would learn technical skills in economics, statistics, and operations research; social science skills to understand and to communicate effectively in political settings; and analytic management skills to improve the nature and quality of public services and the efficiency with which they are produced. The schools varied somewhat in the relative emphasis given to each of these skills, but virtually all required two very intensive years of graduate work leading to a master's degree.

Three hallmarks of this training are quite important to understand. First, the purpose of public policy analysis is to advise decision makers, who are the clients. This purpose distinguishes it from public policy research, which is undertaken for academic reasons (to contribute to knowledge). The term "decision makers" is interpreted broadly: the clients can be citizen-voters in an election, elected public officials or the public managers serving under them, or other stakeholders with legitimate concerns and interests in the policies under consideration. Public policy analysis does not substitute for democratic decision making but informs it in the expectation that more informed decision makers will generally make better policies. But one should not underestimate the creative aspect of informing: devising and presenting a new or modified alternative that may well reconcile conflicting objectives and interests, which has led many to associate policy analysis with problem solving.

Second, the professional responsibility of the public policy analyst is to serve the public interest. The idea is to promote the general welfare or the common good. One aspect of this is to provide objective, factual information about the likely effects of proposed policies on outcomes, even if such information might not be what policy makers wish to hear. This aspect is sometimes referred to as "speaking truth to power" (see Wildavsky 1979). If, for example, government welfare policies are themselves causing people to move out of the workforce and onto welfare and more generous guaranteed-income proposals would exacerbate this, then policy makers must be informed.[2]

Another aspect of serving the public interest is that policy analysts consider the effects of proposed policies on widely shared social goals, like efficiency and equity (fairness). The welfare programs mentioned above were largely undertaken to address fairness concerns, a part of the social safety net. But the work disincentives of these welfare programs were highly distortionary, meaning that they artificially created incentives for many people to reduce their participation in the labor market—an important inefficiency. Recognition of this led analysts to develop new types of welfare assistance that reduced the distortionary work disincentives, notably the earned income tax credit. Thus analysts assisted by improving the design of welfare policies to address both equity and efficiency concerns of policy makers.[3]

This public interest objective distinguishes the professional policy analyst from lobbyists, whose work is to protect and to serve the special interests that they are representing.[4] The public policy analyst looks beyond the interests of any single group or organization to consider policies that best serve the collectivity. This professional responsibility does not mean that the public policy analyst is blind to the interests of a specific client; indeed much policy analytic work involves identifying changes that are both in the public interest and in that of a specific client. This is no different in kind from the responsibilities of many other professionals like doctors, certified public accountants, or actuaries, who must also uphold professional standards and provide objective counsel. Just as physicians will refuse to provide an inappropriate prescription that the patient may have requested, the public policy analyst will not obscure a policy consequence that bears upon the public interest simply because a client may not like it. This professional responsibility is sometimes impressed upon the public policy graduate students by advising them, as they work, to "keep your bags packed" (should a client pressure the analyst to violate professional standards).

The third characteristic of the work of this profession is that it is forward looking: analytic comparisons are about likely future effects of adopting policy alternatives, and recommendations are intended to improve the future. This predictive aspect distinguishes policy analysis from much policy research, which illuminates or evaluates the effects of policies in the past. Of course the latter type of research is often very informative to the practicing policy analyst: it surely helps to know how well or how poorly a policy has been working, and why. But future circumstances are generally different from those in the past, and policy analysis will utilize whatever information is helpful to making predictions about the future effects of policy alternatives under consideration.

The new schools providing training in policy analysis found their graduates in high demand. Initially the demand was largely at the federal level, but it spread quickly to state and local levels as well. Many other universities began to add similar graduate programs, and over time most programs also expanded substantially in size.[5] The Association for Public Policy Analysis and Management (APPAM) was formed in 1979 to promote the intellectual exchange of ideas among the faculties of these schools and practitioners of policy analysis. Since its founding with fifteen institutional members (largely universities but several think tanks as well), APPAM had grown to ninety-five institutional members by 2014.

Of equal importance were the changes occurring in the graduate schools of public administration that predated the policy analysis movement. Beginning in the first half of the twentieth century, these schools trained civil servants, generally emphasizing skill in administrative procedures but not the policy-analytic skills of the new APPAM institutions.[6] The public administration programs belonged to the National Association of Schools of Public Administration and Affairs (NASPAA). In response to the growing demand for policy-analytic training, most NASPAA schools have gradually revised their curricula to offer policy analysis as an option if not a requirement. They have also expanded their training to include the analytic management tools that encourage public managers to lead their agencies in creating services of higher public value and to produce services more efficiently. In 2014, there were 280 NASPAA member schools (some of which are also APPAM members).

Finally, it is important to note that while the modern-day policy-analytic movement had its birth in the United States, it has increasingly spread to countries around the globe. A number of current members of both APPAM and NASPAA are from programs outside of the United States. Indeed, in recognition of the growing globalization of many public policy problems that cannot be addressed by any single country alone (e.g., climate change), NASPAA has recently changed its name to Network of Schools of Public Policy, Affairs and Administration, dropping "National" from its name, and notes that its members are now from fifteen different countries. APPAM, in addition to its annual U.S. conference, sponsors one international conference each year. There are many fine schools of public policy outside of the United States that are not current members of either NASPAA or APPAM.[7]

It is difficult to measure the growth in the use of public policy analysis with any precision. Using data from CBO (2007), I estimate that federal government employment of policy professionals with master's degrees or higher—a group somewhat broader than simply those who have graduated from public policy schools—reached roughly 225,000 by 2005. This number, however, excludes all of the professional analysts employed by state and local governments, the nongovernmental sector, and those outside of the United States.[8]

A different measure of growth is simply the number of schools and programs that produce policy analysts. As a baseline that predates the public policy movement, Henry (1995) reports a U.S. national survey undertaken in 1959–60 that identified approximately one hundred public administration programs with total estimated enrollment of 3,000 graduate students. Henry mentions that almost all of these programs were quite small, many located within traditional political science departments; the average enrollment reported of only 30 students per program is consistent with this. NASPAA was founded in 1970 with 65 member institutions, and as already mentioned that number had grown to 280 by 2014. Of APPAM's institutional members in 2014, only thirteen universities were not also members of NASPAA. So another measure of the growth of the public policy analysis movement is to treat the new members (those above the base of one hundred older programs) as the new public policy programs: the 193 degree-granting programs that largely started after the 1959–60 survey—an average of three to four new university programs per year up to 2014. This understates the growth rate of policy analysis, as it does not include the growth of the policy-analytic curriculum within the hundred base institutions, nor does it count the new programs that have not become APPAM or NASPAA members.

The above measure of institutional growth also does not account directly for the changes in the number of students. Thus a different measure is the annual number of graduate students enrolled in these programs. NASPAA has in recent years been undertaking an annual survey to measure this. It reported 25,120 graduate students enrolled for Fall 2013 classes among 191 responding programs, which averages to 131.52 enrolled per program. This is more than quadruple the enrollments per program in 1959–60, and of course the number of programs is much greater. While there is uncertainty about the total number of these students because not all institutions respond to the surveys, it seems clear that there are at least ten times the number of annual graduate students now than there were in 1959–60.[9] If this annual flow of graduate students turns into jobs at a rate similar to those trained in graduate civil engineering (also primarily a two-year professional degree), then in 2014 we would expect something like 440,000 people trained in public policy analytic skills to be employed and using these skills in the United States.[10]

Not all of these jobs are directly with government. In 2013, NASPAA reported that 51 percent of graduate placements were governmental, 28 percent were in nonprofit agencies, and 21 percent were in private sector agencies.[11] The nonprofit and private sector placements are generally in institutions that advise governments (e.g., think tanks and consulting agencies like RAND, the Urban Institute, Mathematica, MDRC, or Abt Associates) or partner with governments or have other close relationships with governments (e.g., the Ford Foundation, OECD, UNICEF). Thus one does not necessarily need to be employed by government to utilize policy-analytic skills intended to further the public interest.

THE EFFECTS OF THE POLICY ANALYSIS PROFESSION ON POLICY

While analytic resources have grown considerably, they remain small in relation to the value of goods and services that they seek to enhance through better public policies.[12] They remain small in relation to the resources of special interests that also work to influence public policies, typically in different directions. What difference does it make to actual policies to have these highly trained policy analysts working year after year to improve them? This turns out to be a very difficult question to answer, with relatively scant research effort devoted to it. While other essays in this book offer further explanation of the difficulties, new approaches, and some answers, I briefly give an overview here of some of the approaches that researchers have taken and their findings and limitations.

One issue to be kept in mind from the start is that it can be quite difficult to distinguish the effects of scientific knowledge (including social science) on policy making from the effects of public policy professionals, with the latter often playing the roles of translator, broker, creative pragmatist, and opportunist utilizing the scientific knowledge. Many scholars have studied the use of scientific knowledge in policy making more broadly.[13] A report of the National Research Council (Prewitt, Schwandt, and Straf 2012) provides a good overview. We are less interested here in how long it may take for academic research to influence policy than we are in understanding the consequences of active efforts by public policy professionals to use this knowledge in policy making. That said, it is often not possible to separate out the effects of those actually trained in public policy programs from other professionals with whom they may work as part of a network or team, and most work that seeks to understand the effects of public policy professionals does not try to make this distinction.

Probably the most common approach taken to date is the case study, by which I mean a study of one use of policy analysis with no formal comparison to any other ways of using policy analysis. A number of case studies provide good evidence on the effects of public policy analysis. As one example, during most of the twentieth century, the U.S. government restricted entry and regulated the rates charged by the interstate trucking industry. In 1980, the government changed course to deregulate interstate trucking rates and to allow free entry into the industry. Why did this happen, especially given that there were powerful special interests (the trucking firms and the Teamsters' Union) opposed to these changes? Part of the reason is that the analytic case for these changes was compelling, but that was true long before 1980. In her excellent book on this case based on extensive interviews and field observations, Robyn (1987) explains how a dedicated group of public policy analysts working at diverse agencies formed a loose coalition. This coalition worked to ensure that throughout the political process of considering the reform proposal the case made by analysts (and their responses to certain claims made by the special interests) was heard. In an independent retrospective study, Winston (1998) confirms that this deregulation reduced costs in the long run by 35 to 75 percent while increasing service quality.[14] At least in this case, the analytic consensus and the political skills of the analysts made a difference.

A more recent example is the cap-and-trade program instituted by the California Air Resources Board (CARB) to reduce greenhouse gas (GHG) emissions across the state. It is the first cap-and-trade program to include (as of 2015) the emissions from mobile sources (cars and trucks), and these mobile sources account for a very substantial portion (around 40 percent) of California's GHG emissions. The CARB analysts favored the inclusion of all practicable emissions sources within the capped market because this would reduce emissions at the least total cost. However, the powerful motor fuel industry was opposed to being regulated this way, and it fought the proposal during regulatory proceedings and with legislative and legal challenges. Nevertheless, the analytic position prevailed in this instance.[15]

Other case studies involving other policy decisions, like Szanton's (1991) on a federal welfare reform, are similar to the two mentioned above: the outcome was improved because of the inputs from public policy analysts.[16] A problem with such evidence is that no one can be really sure what would have happened without the analytic inputs (absent a formal experimental comparison with random assignment of subjects to either a treatment or a control group). A second problem with this type of evidence, even if the individual cases are very compelling, is that it involves only a minuscule fraction of the analytic efforts made across all public policies. There is certainly no reason to think that the cases are a representative sample of the effects of policy analysis on outcomes. While they may be persuasive enough to establish that policy analysis sometimes achieves its goals, there are also cases of the failure of public policy analytic efforts. An example is offered by Overman and Cahill (1994), who document failed efforts in two states to create useful health data for consumers— data that policy designers and health data experts thought essential for the good functioning of competition in health care provision. The designers and experts were likely correct about the value of good data, but they were off the mark in terms of creating agencies that would produce it. This is a failure of analysis because the policy recommendations were followed but did not lead to the predicted results.

Another failure, at least through 2015, is the largely unheeded calls to control the greenhouse gas emissions that cause global climate change. Whereas California and several other important jurisdictions like the European Union have begun programs to do their part, most of the world has no policies in place so far to make sufficient reductions despite an analytic consensus about the importance of doing so.[17] While scientists have been voicing increasingly strident concerns about greenhouse gas emissions through the Intergovernmental Panel on Climate Change since 1990, this is not quite the same as policy analysts recommending government action. But in 2006 a team of twenty-three governmental analysts from the United Kingdom under the direction of Sir Nicholas Stern called for strong governmental measures to reduce emissions.[18] A number of non-profit organizations with global interests have produced policy analyses evaluating and recommending specific methods of implementing global emissions reductions.[19] While analysts around the world have continued to debate the relative merits of particular approaches for their jurisdictions, they do so now with agreement that substantial global reductions must be mandated and that workable, effective policies can be implemented. Despite the degree of analytic consensus, the world is still far short of the policies necessary to ensure against the possibly catastrophic harm from climate change.

Note that the failure to address global climate change is a different type from the previous example of inadequate health data. The climate change policy failure is that the policy-analytic recommendations have not been followed rather than off-the-mark predictions in the health data example about the usefulness of the resulting data. Of course one might say that the climate change example is a failure of international politics rather than of policy analysis, and it is an unusual case because there is no in-place world government that could implement the recommendations. Nevertheless, to date the substantial policy analytic effort has not resulted in policies carrying out the recommendations for very substantial global emission reductions (no outcome effect). Perhaps the agreement reached at the December 2015 Paris climate conference, signed by 195 nations, will be the breakthrough that leads to the necessary policies. These policies must achieve reductions that are about twice the level of the voluntary pledges that the Paris countries have made.

One might conclude fairly from the case study literature that policy analysis matters sometimes. But is it not possible to know, in a more systematic way, whether there are benefits from public policy analysis that exceed its costs? By "systematic," I refer to research methods that involve formal comparison of one use of policy analysis to another (e.g. perhaps to no policy analysis at all). There are some very clever attempts to provide at least partial answers to this question of systematic effects of policy analysis. Some will be described in more detail in the following chapters. But as a first step here, it is helpful to understand that data limitations constrain the range over which the systematic effects of policy analysis are investigated.

Policy analysis is used in myriad settings, including offices of county, city, regional, state, and federal governments that have no common databases. Some of the best attempts at systematic evaluation examine a large number of public policy decisions, but these are typically in very similar if not the same settings. These natural experiments allow control for all of the uncontrolled factors that might explain why, say, health policy decisions could be more or less influenced by public policy analysis than criminal justice or education policy decisions, or executive branch decisions more than legislative decisions, or federal-level decisions more than county-level decisions. The existing systematic studies generally restrict the setting to a group of decisions that have a common database offering the same information about each of the cases in it, and in which the decisions are made in institutional settings closely related to one another.

One of the earliest systematic attempts is within a specific sector and is by the Nobel Prize–winning economist Daniel McFadden, who studied the highway routing decisions of the California Department of Transportation (McFadden 1975, 1976).

The agency conducted a benefit-cost analysis for each routing decision, had meetings with local officials and public hearings, and then chose a specific route from among the alternatives studied. McFadden examined sixty-five of these decisions; he both made some corrections to the agency's benefit-cost calculations and considered whether or not the route with the greatest net benefits was in fact chosen. His conclusion was that the agency had largely carried out its analytic mission successfully.

While this study is very impressive and served well its purpose of predicting the behavioral choices of the agency, for our purposes it is still subject to some limitations. McFadden had to accept the raw benefit and cost data reported by the agency. He was able to review carefully and critically the steps necessary to make professionally sound benefit-cost calculations from it, but no reviewer could rule out the possibility that some of the agency's raw data might have been biased to some extent—conceivably tilting in the direction of justifying an outcome desired by some special interest. No one has suggested that the latter case is true for any of the decisions in his study, and I raise this here simply as a caution about data used in future research. In other areas such as education reforms that give financial incentives to teachers and schools to improve student performance, some unfortunate instances of data manipulation (i.e., falsified test scores) arose to increase the financial reward.[20]

A much more recent sector-specific study is largely able to overcome the outcome data validity question by the way in which it constructs the data. The study by Anderson, Rauser and Swinnen (2013) uses an impressive data set on worldwide agricultural policies constructed by the World Bank. The annual data set covers the agricultural policies of eighty-two countries spanning the 1955–2010 period, and the study tracks carefully and with quantitative measures how the nature of agricultural policies has changed from year to year in each country and for each of seventy-five different farm products, averaging eleven per country. Before explaining further and discussing some of their findings, some background to relate public policy analysis and agricultural policies is necessary.

I explain in an earlier study (Friedman 1999) why the history of U.S. agricultural policy might be of high value to those interested in understanding the effectiveness of public policy analysis. I focus on the many U.S. agricultural subsidy programs that have costs to ordinary citizens much greater than benefits and that have been shown neither to make farm incomes more stable nor to target the benefits to poor farmers who might be deserving of assistance on fairness or equity grounds. Most of these programs started through New Deal legislation in response to the Great Depression. A key characteristic they share is that they distort prices from those that would exist under normal competition. Indeed, economists have argued at least since the 1940s that such programs are poor policies and that they should be eliminated. But instead the programs generally expanded in size and thus in their inefficiency, at least up through about 1980.

The persistence of these programs over such a lengthy period presents an analytic puzzle. Becker (1983) was the first to raise the persistence of inefficient policies as a puzzle. The definition of economic inefficiency means that it is possible to alter the resource allocation such that the gains to the gainers exceed the losses to the losers. Therefore it is possible by eliminating the inefficiency for the gainers to compensate the losers so that everyone comes out ahead. Some have argued, for the agricultural case, that political power explains the persistence of inefficiency. The farmers gaining from the inefficient programs are concentrated and represented by well-organized and well-paid lobbyists. The ordinary citizens who bear the much greater aggregate costs are many and diffuse, with each individual only losing a relatively small amount and thus lacking incentive to organize politically. But this political power argument does not resolve Becker's puzzle, because the well-organized farmers themselves have incentives to offer proposals that would remove the inefficiency and more than compensate them for doing so.

Note that if Becker's model is essentially correct, it removes one of the primary reasons for having public policy analysts. There would be no policy inefficiencies left to improve. It implies that the case of trucking inefficiency under regulation reviewed above would not have existed. But of course we do observe continuing inefficiencies in many public policies, and ameliorating or eliminating them is one of the main tasks of the policy analysis profession.

In my 1999 work I extended Becker's logic to include significant information and transaction costs that help to explain the persistence of inefficiency. It is very difficult to figure out an implementable policy that removes the existing inefficiency, that will be considered by decision makers who already have very busy agendas, and that satisfies enough of the policy stakeholders (e.g,. includes a credible commitment to compensate losers) that the proposal will have sufficient support to be politically adopted. These substantial information and transaction costs create a type of "status quo" bias. Friedman highlights the crucial role of public policy analysts in overcoming these information and transaction costs. At least in some cases, the power of their policy ideas (and their amendments to those proposed by others) as well as their political skills may be just enough to overcome the status quo bias and lead to policy improvements.

Examining U.S. agricultural policies, I document that they start to gradually become less inefficient in 1985. Three major farm bills were undertaken during the scope of my study: the 1985 Food Security Act; the 1990 Food, Agriculture, Conservation and Trade Act; and the 1996 Federal Agriculture Improvement and Reform Act. While each allowed some of the existing inefficiencies to continue, each chipped away at some of the price-distortionary policies and replaced them with less distortionary ones, generally compensating the affected farmers with nondistortionary assistance.

The study by Anderson, Rausser, and Swinnen (2013) documents more formally, more broadly, and more continually the steady, incremental improvement in agricultural policies that I hypothesized one should expect if policy analysis matters. They construct several continuous measures of inefficiency, including one called the welfare reduction index, or WRI, which is the percentage uniform tax that if applied to all of a country's tradable agricultural output would cause the same degree of inefficiency as the actual policies in place for those goods.[21] The higher the constructed tax rate, the greater the inefficiency of the public policies. They provide this measure for a group of countries termed "high-income" (Western Europe, the United States, Canada, Japan, Australia, and New Zealand) and show that it drops dramatically and continuously from a level of over 80 percent in the 1980–85 period to under 30 percent by 2010.[22] This study provides one of the most useful, comprehensive measures of change in the quality of public policies that apply to that area. It would certainly be of value to have similar indexes developed in other policy areas, such as for health care provision, housing, or regulated utility service.

This study has the great strength of being able to provide a key measure of how the quality of agricultural policies has been changing over time. However, it neither proves nor disproves whether any portion of the change is due to public policy analysts. It is simply highly suggestive that the improvements did not occur before there were good numbers of policy analysts; indeed, in the earlier era largely without them (1960–85) the quality was generally decreasing over time. But there are other important factors that could be contributing to the observed trends. Indeed, a good part of Anderson, Rausser, and Swinnen's study is devoted to a review of possible political economy reasons (e.g., shifting power of interest groups) that help to explain the trends. Still, there is no inconsistency in both being important factors.[23]

The discussion so far has focused on the direct effects of policy analyses on policy outcomes. But the indirect effects could be substantial. On the positive side, they could be very valuable. Even without conducting an analysis, a process in which those trained in policy analysis participate could have an important effect on the nature of policy arguments made by various parties. There could be a tendency for better evidence to be put forth over poorer evidence, knowing that the poorer evidence is unlikely to stand up to analytic scrutiny.[24] With a good number of participants in the process who have analytic training, more effort by all to improve their use of evidence would be a natural consequence. It is quite possible that the presence of nonpartisan analysts will lead constituents to value the whole process more highly. Participants and other interested parties may have better alternatives, understand better the consequences of choosing one over the others, and appreciate the legitimacy of policy-analytic efforts to contribute to this process. It can make it more difficult for forces of cronyism or corruption to influence the process.

But on the negative side of possible indirect effects, analysts might take away from or substitute for what otherwise would be a legitimate democratic process. While clearly not the profession's intent, the use of expertise could inadvertently substitute for legitimate democratic expression. This could happen, for example, if there is limited time for presentations during legislative hearings and if more of that time is given to nonpartisan analysts and less to stakeholder groups.

In fact, the legislative setting for policy analysis may raise more issues than its use within executive branch settings, precisely because the legislature is intended to be the institution for the clash of democratic forces—setting it apart from the primarily management function of the executive branch and, for that matter, the judicial branch.[25] Several systematic studies of the effects of policy analysis in legislatures have shown that democratic process effects are important.

Shulock (1999) considers indirect process effects in the federal legislative setting, where some studies have reported little to no direct effects of policy analyses on the legislative outcomes.[26] She offers the "better process" argument and subjects it to empirical testing in the legislative setting, using the 105 House Committee reports on "key vote" bills in the 1985–94 period.[27] She finds that there is significantly greater use of policy analysis (measured by citation counts in the reports) by legislative committees when there are multiple committees involved in considering the legislation. Multiple committees compete to have primary responsibility for framing the issue and to have the major role in drafting the legislation. There is no reason to expect more use of policy analysis in this context if the only role of analysis is to clarify substantive effects of policy alternatives. But one would expect it if the analysis provides a boost to the perceived expertise of the committee utilizing it, thus increasing its chances of playing leading roles for that legislation as well as related legislation. This is consistent with policy analysis contributing by making the process of deciding more evidence based and more transparent, with heightened legitimacy.

Hird (2005) provides an extensive systematic examination of the use of policy analysis in state legislatures. While direct effects of policy analyses in those settings do not appear to be strong, there does appear to be substantial evidence supporting the Shulock thesis that the practice of policy analysis by nonpartisan legislative research agencies improves the overall process. Such agencies are widely acknowledged for their political neutrality, excel at providing relevant information, and thus make the process more evidence based. Hird emphasizes the importance of the interpersonal trust relationship with frequent contact between legislators and policy analysts: the analytical people matter, not simply the content of written documents. In addition, Hird's evidence is inconsistent with the possibility that policy analysis might devalue the democratic process in state legislatures. He shows instead how the demands of the state political system have had a large impact in terms of shaping what the policy analysts do—resulting in analytic emphasis on the short-term problems that preoccupy the legislators, on nonpartisan information provision under tight time deadlines so it is available as needed, and on minimizing use of their skill as creative problem solvers in order to maintain their strict neutrality in this politically dynamic setting.

The systematic studies mentioned above raise interesting questions about the effects of policy analysis in different settings and suggest reasons to expect variation across them. This leads to a final approach to investigating the effects of policy analysis that has different strengths and weaknesses. A quite different method of establishing the value of an activity comes from economics and is generally held in high regard: the market test in terms of voluntary purchasing of the activity, in this case the hiring of public policy graduates. When people buy something, it is generally because the value to them of the purchase is at least equal to its cost. Employers are not in the habit of knowingly hiring employees who do not provide value at least equal to their salary and benefit costs. Just as we assume that employed civil engineers are creating value greater than their cost through their work on the design, construction, and maintenance of roads, bridges, and buildings, the same must be true for public policy professionals. If neither civil engineers nor public policy professionals were creating this value, then employers would reduce their employment of them until left with the smaller group that can pull its own weight.

I do not wish to overstate this argument. Of course a single organization at a single point in time may make errors and find itself with too many or too few public policy professionals and adjust accordingly. There may be instances of a government requiring policy analysis that should not have been undertaken because of, say, inadequate data; it is likely that such a government would learn from its mistake and reduce the instances of this in the future. But the fact that over the past half century employers have continued to hire increasing numbers of public policy professionals is, in fact, a crucial demonstration of their high value.[28]

Some might object to this reasoning by pointing out that governmental services do not take place in a true, voluntary market setting. There is some merit to this objection in certain circumstances, but I do not think it applies in this case. The Becker logic reviewed earlier, of strong political competition tending to drive out any long-run inefficiency, applies. In the U.S. context, as well as in many other countries, there is actually extraordinary competition across governments and within governments for resources. There is never enough money to pay for all of the schooling, health care, infrastructure, defense, and other services demanded by constituents. If professional policy analysts were not actually pulling their weight in terms of helping to stretch the existing governmental resources, there are plenty of political leaders who would gain by not hiring more of them and using the same money to provide other valued governmental services like more forest rangers, teachers, and transportation engineers. The fact that the number of professional policy analysts has increased greatly over time, in diverse governmental and nongovernmental agencies, despite the importance of other competing needs, is itself persuasive evidence that their value— their positive effect in terms of improving the governmental goods and services that they analyze—exceeds their cost.

Another feature of this market test is worth pointing out. I have emphasized several times the very broad range of governmental services that policy analysts work to improve and the many types of employers that can utilize their services (governments at all levels, nonprofit organizations, and private sector institutions that advise governments). This creates a great research difficulty when trying to measure direct effects of policy analysis on such a wide variety of governmental services, especially when there may be important differences from one setting to another in terms of the capability of policy analysis to contribute. The market test to some extent reveals these differences; for example, if it is harder for policy analysts to contribute to education services than to health-related services, then we would expect proportionately fewer policy analysts to be working in the educational policy field (controlling for the relative sector sizes). To my knowledge, this has not been investigated, but it could certainly be interesting to do so. Finally, note that the market test provides evidence of value across all of the diverse sectors and settings in which policy analysts work. Thus it has an advantage over the systematic methods that must be restricted to a narrower area in order to have good measures of the direct effects of the policy-analytic work on outcomes.

The market test of employment causes us to appreciate the diversity of organizational settings to which policy analysts can contribute or add social value. There are also a multitude of different ways in which analysts enhance the social value of our public policies. Understanding these different ways helps us to recognize their contributions. One way to conceptualize these ways is by identifying the different steps involved in public problem solving, with the understanding that each step is important in achieving a solution. The steps are usually taught in introductory policy analysis courses, and most policy analysts are trained in all of them. Major ones include problem definition, identification of alternative possible solutions, specification of criteria for judging how well an alternative performs, the acquisition and use of data to project the consequences of each alternative, evaluation of the consequences by the criteria, confronting the trade-offs among criteria, coming to a recommendation, and effective communication of the work to the clients or decision makers.[29]

Scholars of policy analysis have long recognized that different analysts may have different relative strengths among the different steps and may concentrate or specialize their work accordingly. But specialization only works when one is part of a network or team in which other members have responsibility for the missing or lightly treated steps in the work of the specialist.

Some analysts are brilliant at understanding and marshaling empirical evidence, generally to project a policy's consequences, but they may shy away from the type of political communication that is necessary to convey their work effectively. Another analyst may be a truly gifted writer who excels at explaining analytic work in a report or memo that clients will find clear and persuasive. Still another may be a creative whiz who thinks of stunning new practical alternatives that did not occur to others. And another might be a master at understanding how governmental bureaucracies will likely implement any specific idea and thus be able to make better projections of actual consequences and avoid alternatives that will have unintended adverse consequences. Still another will be a great oral communicator, with the ability to understand diverse political interests and increase support for good policy proposals.

Thus different analysts will have different skill levels for each of the problem-solving steps, and each will contribute in somewhat different ways to the overall goal of improving public policies. Generally the organizations that hire them will understand the relative strengths of each and will try to have a group of analysts that together form an effective team. In some cases, one organization may coordinate its efforts with that of another organization to develop the full problem-solving capacity that some problems may demand.

Understanding the different ways that analysts may add to social value provides a further tool for assessing effectiveness. I referred earlier to the "direct effects" of policy analysis, which in the problem-solving terminology means reaching a better solution than would have been reached without policy analysis. The degree of "better" can sometimes be measured as the dollar benefits, like the higher economic value of the better routes chosen due to the analysis of the California Department of Transportation or the tax savings equivalent from analysis that leads to more efficient agricultural policies. But at least to this point studies with such measures have been rare. I also referred earlier to the "indirect effects" of policy analysis, which in the problem-solving terminology means an improved or more highly valued public problem-solving process. An example would be a nonpartisan state legislative analyst's office that provides more accurate information to the legislature about the policies that are under consideration.

In cases where determination of the direct effects is difficult, it may be possible to determine if there are significant contributions in terms of the indirect effects. That is, it may be possible to observe if any of the problem-solving steps are being carried out better (or worse) due to the presence of analysts. While a better problem-solving step is not as conclusive as measuring the actual change in outcome, it is like finding out that the probability of selecting a better outcome has increased. In any one case the outcome may or may not be better, but over many cases the law of large numbers implies that on average better policy outcomes will result. In other words, the same problem-solving steps that reveal how individual analysts may add social value may also be used as a framework for assessing if a policy-making process has been improved.

Summing up this section, there is a lot of evidence that public policy analysis matters. Detailed case studies of the roles of specific policy analyses in the policy-making process provide evidence that, at least sometimes, the analytic efforts have made important differences to the outcomes. More systematic studies in some areas like transportation and agriculture, looking at the effects of regularly undertaking policy analyses in those areas, have found that the policy outcomes do seem to be improved. This has not been the case for those studies that have examined the use of policy analysis in legislative settings, where they report little to no direct effects on outcomes. But even in the legislative settings, there seems to be mounting evidence that nonpartisan policy analysis is providing important value in another way: it is making the process of deciding more evidence based, more transparent, and perhaps more respected. The different steps of public problem solving provide a useful framework for assessing if a policy-making process has been improved. Finally, because those who are trained in the skills of policy analysis and public management have been hired in rapidly growing numbers over the past fifty years, this market test indicates that their skills have been and continue to be highly valued over the very wide range of institutions that employ them and that this value at least exceeds their costs.

Even with this positive evidence, there are good reasons to wonder about the effectiveness of policy analysis in all of its applications. There are case studies and examples where the analytic efforts have not been successful, and these may provide important clues to improve the profession's effectiveness. It can be difficult, in some circumstances, to distinguish between the failure of policy analysis and the success of democracy. Independently of its direct effects on policy outcomes, policy analysis may be having important effects on the value of governmental decision processes—and this certainly deserves further study. There may also be some policy areas that are systematically more responsive to analytic effort and others that are less so. Progress in terms of how we measure direct policy outcomes as well as evaluate process changes might lead to new understandings of the effectiveness of public policy professionals.

TOWARD FURTHER UNDERSTANDING OF THE EFFECTS OF POLICY ANALYSIS IN PRACTICE

I have alluded to the idea that policy analysis is undertaken in many different types of policy-making settings and by different stakeholders that participate in those settings. This occurs at local, state, and federal levels of government, and policy analysis is used by each level's legislative bodies and executive branch departments and agencies. Policy analysis also gets presented and examined in judicial settings and is used by the judicial branch to improve the effectiveness of court operations. Policy analysis is undertaken at times for citizen-voters directly, for example, as material available to voters in an initiative process. So when we ask whether policy analysis matters, there is a lot of territory to cover.

The size of the overall puzzle that would need to be put together to give a comprehensive answer to our question is well beyond the scope of this volume. Indeed, solving such a puzzle implies a research agenda that will take many years and many different scholars using many different approaches to carry out. Building on the existing research and contributing to it, each of the following chapters in this volume picks one relatively small area of the overall puzzle and offers some illumination in that area. In introducing these below, I offer a view of the parts to which I see each chapter contributing. I hope this will help to keep each chapter in perspective and perhaps serve as a placeholder for the other parts deserving of future scrutiny.

Policy Analysis in the Regulatory Setting

Within the executive branch of the U.S. government, policy decisions are made on myriad subjects that affect the country's citizens, and all of these may be scrutinized through policy analysis.
These decisions range from national defense, space exploration,
and highway safety to forms of welfare assistance, allowed medic-
inal drugs, and so on. Some of these decisions are about services
directly provided by the federal government, for example, the size
of our naval fleet and the specific locations of its deployment.
Other federal decisions affect goods and services provided by
other governments, for example, intergovernmental grants within
the United States that promote new methods of policing, library
services, or K–12 education or foreign assistance to promote U.S.
aims abroad. The effectiveness of these programs depends not just
on the quality of federal oversight and management, but on how
the receiving governments choose to respond to them (and therefore their preferences, analyses, and management). A third broad
category of federal decisions, in addition to direct service provision and intergovernmental programs, encompasses regulatory
decisions: decisions that affect private firms and individuals by
limiting in some way the scope of their activities, for example,
health and safety standards for workplaces or air pollution limits
that affect how electric power is generated. The effects of federal
regulatory decisions will therefore depend on how the regulated
entities respond to the regulations.

Chapter 2, by John Hird, discusses the effectiveness of policy
analysis generally and then focuses on its use in the federal regulatory setting. It emphasizes that there are quite different definitions of *policy analysis,* ranging from almost any social science
that discusses a policy to a tightly focused analysis of alternative

policies evaluated and compared by public interest criteria leading to a specific recommendation. Effectiveness can also be
defined broadly, from almost any use that is made of the policy
research to whether or not the analysis improves the outcome of
the policy-making process as judged by public interest criteria.
Hird clarifies the import of these alternative definitions and
reviews the sparse literature that has attempted to assess effectiveness by these definitions.

He then presents research on the effects of policy analyses in
federal regulatory impact analyses. This is a particularly interesting institutional setting, as most of the formal steps of a policy
analysis are required by executive order for all major new federal
regulations. One of his findings is that there is quite substantial use
of social science research in these analyses and furthermore that
higher-quality research as evidenced by publication in top journals is utilized more extensively than research on the same subject
published elsewhere. However, the written documentation of analysis in the federal regulatory setting is exceptional. Hird also finds
that while policy analysts are many, in most areas they are rarely
expected to produce the type of analyses that are envisioned in
any of the policy analysis textbooks and explains why.

Policy Analysis in Specific Institutions:
The U.S. Congress

Federal executive branch decisions are made to carry out the
lawful duties and responsibilities of the federal government, but
these duties and responsibilities change over time. A primary
method for deciding these changes is through congressional
deliberation and enactment of legislation. While Congress does
not have the management responsibilities of the executive

branch, its elected members represent a broad diversity of regions and political philosophies that make it challenging, to say the least, to come to any agreement on legislation. Its deliberations can be quite controversial, such as the use of a filibuster by a member who wishes to obstruct the progression of a proposed bill. Its deliberations do not arise from within one administration implementing existing law (the executive branch) but instead from the abutting of pluralistic forces in which the vision or voice of one group may be quite at odds with that of another. Perhaps it should be expected that nonpartisan policy analysis will have more difficulty expressing its voice in this type of setting.

Chapter 3, by Eric Patashnik and Justin Peck, addresses this legislative setting explicitly. While professional policy analysis began within the executive branch of the U.S. government, its use spread to Congress through different venues like congressional staff and agencies like the Congressional Research Service, the Congressional Budget Office, and the Government Accountability Office. Patashnik and Peck criticize some of the earlier studies that assess congressional use of policy analysis for applying too narrow a conception of how analysis can affect decision making. They conduct an original survey of over 150 policy professionals working in the Washington, DC, area and use it to assess how well Congress carries out the different tasks or steps of policy analysis. That is, similar to chapter 2, they ask how well a certain institution carries out the policy-analytic mission rather than viewing policy analysis as the task of an individual or a small team focused on one particular issue. They present a richly nuanced view of their findings, which involves substantial new criticisms of congressional "rationality" but also some praise for accomplishments on the accountability side of the relationship between legislators and the citizens they represent. They also offer suggestions for improving the process so that Congress can improve its use of policy analysis.

Policy Analysis and Implementation:
Service-Providing Public Agencies

In all countries, including the United States, there are a host of important public services that are delivered at the level of localities: police protection, fire protection, education, libraries, refuse collection and recycling, and so on. Countries vary in terms of the institutions used to deliver these services, but they almost always have the characteristic that the delivery in some localities differs from the delivery of the same service in other localities. To some extent, these differences may reflect the very reasons the delivery is local: to fit the varying preferences and circumstances that may characterize the different localities. But the difference may also be due in part to variations in how well each locality is performing the given task. Indeed, the importance of "best practices" research and its dissemination is precisely because it may be quite difficult for each locality to learn the best way to deliver the service in its own local context.

My work examining how pretrial services are delivered in local criminal justice systems throughout the United States documents wide performance variation (Friedman 1997). It is not simply that there is variation across the localities; there is also strong variation over time within particular localities. New York City adopted the reform I studied and initially used it with a high degree of success. But over time, the initial success gradually withered away such that by the end of the period studied the entire operation was ineffective. However, there was no similar evidence of deterioration in Washington, DC, where the same reform was also adopted. Friedman (1997) found that some localities adopted the reform and improved their performance over time, while other localities' performance deteriorated over time. What explains these performance variations, and what can be done to improve performance levels for these locally delivered types of services?

The U.S. and other national governments spend considerable resources to improve these local services. They conduct research, identify promising new innovative methods, and sponsor pilot projects, often subjecting them to evaluation through rigorous controlled experiments. For those new ideas that are proven to work and to offer substantial improvements, the national governments generally encourage their diffusion to the localities through policy instruments. These instruments vary from information dissemination to grants that offer financial incentives to the adopting localities and in a few cases to mandated adoption (as with new standards for firefighters' protective equipment that takes advantage of technological innovations, or new performance standards for schools in the 2001 No Child Left Behind legislation). But are these policy instruments sufficient to induce the local learning that may be critical to high performance implementation?

This question is the subject of chapter 4, by Suzanne Donovan. Donovan considers the practice of policy analysis for the service-providing agencies of government like schools and assesses how well suited the policy-analytic tools are to being a source of improved policies for these agencies. Her assessment draws on some twenty-plus years of experience studying and implementing policies to improve schooling. Her focus on this part of government brings us back naturally to one of the early lessons of policy analysis: the way in which policies actually get implemented is a crucial determinant of their success or failure.

Donovan's central idea of design goes well beyond any simple conception of implementation. She views the operating agencies as being always constrained by their existing base of knowledge and skills, always capable through learning of how to operate better, and always faced with opportunities that will require organizational learning. The central issue for Donovan is how to recognize when the capability of the school system must be improved ("the complex") in order to be commensurate with the ideas for educational improvement that it is asked to implement, and how to do so. Policy analysis that leads to new performance standards (e.g., No Child Left Behind) or other incentives to improve performance but does not routinely consider how to build in the capability for improvement that will be necessary for successful implementation can make the system worse rather than better. She describes how the concept of system design as a component of policy analysis can be used to address this complexity issue and thereby increase the effectiveness of the analysis.

Each of the essays in this book is designed to make us think better and harder about how to improve the practice and use of policy analysis. We consider what we have learned so far about whether and how policy analysis matters, how this learning helps to generate ideas for improving practice, and why learning more about this is an important agenda for future research.

NOTES

1. See www.rand.org/about/history/a-brief-history-of-rand.html.

2. Friedman (2002, 108–10) discusses the work disincentives of some welfare programs, particularly when the same household qualified for more than one of them. In the 1960s and 1970s, there were several congressional bills proposing various forms of guaranteed income, such as

the Family Assistance Plan proposed during the Nixon administration. They did not pass due to a variety of concerns, including work disincentives.

3. Many public policy issues raise difficult value trade-offs for which the analyst has no special expertise to reconcile, and in such cases the analyst informs decision makers about the nature of these trade-offs. An important component of public policy graduate training is learning about different conceptions of the public interest, understanding that different decision makers will often have different understandings of it, and how the objective work of the analysts can be most helpful to the decision process. Welfare programs often cause some change in the amount that the recipient works. How policy makers regard such changes may well depend on the characteristics of the recipients. For example, the recipients might be single parents of infants for whom policy makers intend to increase the parental time at home. Alternatively, the recipients might be out-of-school adults working part-time with no dependents, for whom policymakers intend to stimulate increased work effort.

4. There is nothing inherently wrong with lobbying. Lobbying often can work to convey important information about the consequences of proposed or actual policies that might otherwise have been missed and to suggest innovative new policies. Lobbyists may be the means by which groups that have a right to express themselves do so. An important question is whether all such groups have not only the right but also the means to express themselves adequately. Industries dominated by a few large corporations may have no trouble making their concerns known through lobbying, whereas there may be millions of consumers of the goods and services of these industries who do not have the means to organize and express their common concerns. One response to this situation is found in California, where its Public Utilities Commission has created the Intervenor Compensation Program that will, under certain specified conditions and limits, pay the fees of those representing consumer groups. More information about this program may be found on its website: www.cpuc.ca.gov /PUC/IntervenorCompGuide/.

5. Radin (2013) provides an excellent description of how the training in these public policy schools has evolved over time.

6. The first graduate professional degree in public administration was offered by the Maxwell School of Syracuse University, founded in 1924.

7. For example, the National Graduate Institute for Policy Studies in Japan or Public Policy programs in the United Kingdom at the University of Oxford, London School of Economics and Political Science, and University College London.

8. The U.S. Census does not provide occupational or employment data that are refined enough to be restricted to this profession. CBO (2007) reports on the number of salaried full-time permanent federal employees, of which there were 1.22 million in 1975, with 26.7 percent of them, or 325,740, classified as professionals having master's degrees or higher. Professionals include accountants, lawyers, engineers and others, so for purposes of this estimate I will assume that there were no policy professionals among them in 1975. CBO (2007) also reports that these numbers had grown to 1.44 million, with a dramatic increase to 42.2 percent, or 607,680, classified as professionals with master's degrees or higher in 2005. I assume that the (overestimated) non-policy professionals in the 1975 group grew by the same 18 percent (to 384,480) as all full-time salaried federal employees and that only the excess growth above that of 223,200 is the number of policy professionals in the group.

9. There is a fairly high number of nonrespondents, including both smaller and larger programs. It is not known how the respondents and nonrespondents differ. Nevertheless, certain reasonable conclusions may be drawn. If the missing institutions (89 NASPAA members and 13 non-NASPAA and APPAM members) were similar in size to the respondents, that would imply total enrollment of 38,535. If the missing institutions were half the size of the respondents, that would imply total enrollment of 31,827. Within this range, there are still more than ten times the number of graduate students than there were in 1959–60.

10. Substantially less than half of these 440,000 people are employed by the federal government. The earlier estimate of 225,000 federally employed policy professionals in 2005 includes those with graduate degrees other than from public policy programs. It would include, for example, some with master's degrees from the related fields of urban planning, civil engineering, and business, as well as

some PhDs from a variety of fields like economics. The 440,000 estimate of practicing policy professionals employed in the United States and possessing master's degrees from the public policy schools is derived as follows. The Bureau of Labor Statistics reports that in 2012 there were 272,900 civil engineering jobs, and the National Science Foundation reports that in 2011 there were 19,596 civil engineering graduate students, for a jobs/students ratio of 13.93. This already takes into account that not all those trained in civil engineering end up employed as civil engineers. Applying this same ratio to our lower estimate of 31,827 public policy graduate students, this implies roughly 440,000 employees with these skills. Use of our lower estimate may give an estimate that is too low, but this will be offset to the extent that the annual number of public policy students trained was growing faster than the number of civil engineering students trained (i.e., there may be fewer "older" public policy employees relative to the number of "older" civil engineers).

11. This was reported as one of the results of NASPAA's 2012–2013 Annual Program Survey and appears in a presentation titled "AY 2012–2013 Annual Program Survey Results" on its website: www.naspaa.org/DataCenter/index.asp.

12. In 2015 total expenditures by federal, state, and local governments came to $5.9 trillion, and the heavily regulated private sectors of the economy represent another $2–3 trillion. The analytic resources, valued at an average salary of $75,000, are less than one-half of one percent of this.

13. Examples are Aaron (1978), Featherman and Vinovskis (2001), Lindblom and Cohen (1979), and Rich (2001). For an excellent recent summary, see chapter 4 of Conlan, Posner, and Beam 2014.

14. See Winston 1998, table 3, p. 101.

15. For more on this example, see Friedman 2010.

16. A recent book on this general theme is Haskins and Margolis 2015, presenting six case studies from the Obama administration of social policy areas where analytic perseverance to require use of the best evidence improved policy design and policy implementation.

17. A very promising agreement was signed by 195 countries at the Paris climate conference in December 2015, in which they pledged to work together to keep any increase in global average temperature to well

below 2 degrees centigrade. However, the specific policies necessary to achieve this goal have yet to be formalized and implemented, and it may take many years before it is known if this agreement will lead to the realization of the goal. The reduction pledges offered by the signatory countries total to less than half those necessary to achieve the goal.

18. This is commonly referred to as the Stern Report. See Stern 2007.

19. See, for example, the World Resources Institute 2010 report examining the existing emission reduction pledges of developed countries and recommending deeper cuts to be taken in response to the December 2009 Copenhagen Accord (Levin and Bradley 2010). As another example, see the 2014 report *Better Growth, Better Climate* from the Global Commission on the Economy and Climate urging countries to enter an international climate agreement, available at http://2014 .newclimateeconomy.report/wp-content/uploads/2014/08/NCE-Global-Report_web.pdf.

20. For example, eleven Atlanta teachers were convicted of racketeering by falsifying student test results in order to collect bonuses or to keep their jobs. See the Associated Press article by Kate Brumback on April 2, 2015, at http://bigstory.ap.org/article/58447a404ff34413be53 6de642a38a99/former-atlanta-educators-jailed-test-cheating-scandal.

21. Friedman (1999) suggested such a measure: "The dependent variable would be a continuous efficiency measure, like the change in deadweight loss per crop" (22).

22. See Anderson, Rausser, and Swinnen 2013, fig. 4, p. 433.

23. Rodrik (2014) recognizes this explicitly and argues that more focus on the power of ideas and the roles of policy analysis would strengthen political economy models.

24. This does not mean that no poor evidence would ever be presented. It is not always easy for political participants to recognize these limitations. In some cases, the self-interest of a participant may cause it to try to offer some justification for its policy position if there is a chance that the weakness in its argument will not come to light.

25. The executive branch like the legislature also has many responsibilities in the democratic process; for example, it is often the originator of proposed new legislation that will be considered by the legislature. But its main job is to carry out its legal responsibilities by implementing and managing the policies and programs that do so. A

president may well consider proposing new legislation that affects, say, veterans, but that president also continues to be responsible every day for the oversight and management of all activities of the U.S. Department of Veterans Affairs.

26. Policy analysts may still help to create innovative policies, as they did in 1989 when the Bush administration decided to include in its proposed amendments to the Clean Air Act a cap-and-trade program for sulfur dioxide emissions that then won legislative approval. See Hausker 1992. See chapter 3 in this volume by Patashnik and Peck for further review and investigation of policy analysis in the federal legislative setting.

27. The *Congressional Quarterly Almanac* identifies sixteen votes each year as "key" House votes.

28. When the number hired per year is no longer growing but stabilizes at a level just sufficient to replace those who have separated from the workplace (e.g., due to retirement), that would be the "equilibrium" quantity of public policy professionals; numbers above this level, as judged by employers, would not be able to pull their own weight.

29. For a fuller exposition of these, see the excellent textbooks Weimer and Vining 2016 and Bardach and Patashnik 2016.

REFERENCES

Aaron, Henry. 1978. *Politics and the Professors: The Great Society in Perspective.* Washington, DC: Brookings Institution.

Anderson, Kym, Gordon Rausser, and Johan Swinnen. 2013. "Political Economy of Public Policies: Insights from Distortions to Agricultural and Food Markets." *Journal of Economic Literature* 51, no. 2 (June): 423–77.

Bardach, Eugene, and Eric M. Patashnik. 2016. *A Practical Guide for Policy Analysis: The Eightfold Path to More Effective Problem Solving.* 5th ed. Thousand Oaks, CA: CQ Press.

Becker, Gary. 1983. "A Theory of Competition among Pressure Groups for Political Influence." *Quarterly Journal of Economics* 98 (3): 371–400.

Congressional Budget Office (CBO). 2007. *Characteristics and Pay of Federal Civilian Employees.* March. Washington, DC: CBO.

Conlan, T., P. Posner, and D. Beam. 2014. *Pathways of Power: The Dynamics of National Policymaking.* Washington, DC: Georgetown University Press.

Featherman, David, and Maris Vinovskis. 2001. *Social Science and Policy-Making.* Ann Arbor: University of Michigan Press.

Friedman, Lee. 1997. "Public Sector Innovations and Their Diffusion: Economic Tools and Managerial Tasks." In A. Altshuler and R. Behn, eds., *Innovation in American Government,* 332–59. Washington, DC: Brookings Institution Press.

———. 1999. "Presidential Address: Peanuts Envy?" *Journal of Policy Analysis and Management* 18, no. 2 (Spring): 211–25.

———. 2002. *The Microeconomics of Public Policy Analysis.* Princeton, NJ: Princeton University Press.

———. 2010. "Should California Include Motor Vehicle Fuel Emissions in a Greenhouse Gas Cap-and-Trade Program?" *Journal of Comparative Policy Analysis* 12, no. 3 (June): 217–50.

Haskins, Ron, and Greg Margolis. 2015. *Show Me the Evidence: Obama's Fight for Rigor and Results in Social Policy.* Washington, DC: Brookings Institution Press.

Hausker, Karl. 1992. "The Politics and Economics of Auction Design in the Market for Sulfur Dioxide Pollution." *Journal of Policy Analysis and Management* 11, no. 4 (Fall): 553–72.

Henry, Laurin. 1995. "Early NASPAA History." Available at www.naspaa.org/about_naspaa/about/history.asp.

Hird, John A. 2005. *Power, Knowledge, and Politics: Policy Analysis in the States.* Washington, DC: Georgetown University Press.

Levin, Kelly, and Rob Bradley. 2010. "Comparability of Annex I Emission Reduction Pledges." WRI Working Paper, World Resources Institute, Washington DC, February. Available at www.wri.org.

Lindblom, Charles, and David Cohen. 1979. *Usable Knowledge: Social Science and Social Problem Solving.* New Haven, CT: Yale University Press.

McFadden, Daniel. 1975. "The Revealed Preferences of a Government Bureaucracy: Theory." *Bell Journal of Economics* 6, no. 2 (Autumn): 401–16.

———. 1976. "The Revealed Preferences of a Government Bureaucracy: Empirical Evidence." *Bell Journal of Economics* 7, no. 1 (Spring): 55–72.

Overman, E. Sam, and Anthony Cahill. 1994. "Information, Market Government, and Health Policy: A Study of Health Data Organizations in the States." *Journal of Policy Analysis and Management* 13, no. 3 (Summer): 435–53.

Prewitt, Kenneth, Thomas Schwandt, and Miron Straf, eds. 2012. *Using Science as Evidence in Public Policy.* Washington, DC: National Research Council, National Academies Press.

Radin, Beryl. 2013. *Beyond Machiavelli: Policy Analysis Reaches Midlife.* 2nd ed. Washington, DC: Georgetown University Press.

Rich, Robert. 2001. *Social Science Information and Public Policy Making.* New Brunswick, NJ: Transaction Publishing.

Robyn, Dorothy. 1987. *Braking the Special Interests: Trucking Deregulation and the Politics of Policy Reform.* Chicago: University of Chicago Press.

Rodrik, Dani. 2014. "When Ideas Trump Interests: Preferences, Worldviews, and Policy Innovations." *Journal of Economic Perspectives* 28, no. 1 (Winter): 189–208.

Shulock, Nancy. 1999. "The Paradox of Policy Analysis: If It Is Not Used, Why Do We Produce So Much of It?" *Journal of Policy Analysis and Management* 18, no. 2 (Spring): 226–44.

Stern, Nicholas. 2007. *The Economics of Climate Change: The Stern Review.* Cambridge: Cambridge University Press.

Szanton, Peter. 1991. "The Remarkable 'Quango': Knowledge, Politics, and Welfare Reform." *Journal of Policy Analysis and Management* 10, no. 4 (Autumn): 590–602.

Weimer, David L., and Aidan R. Vining. 2016. *Policy Analysis: Concepts and Practice.* 5th ed. New York: Routledge.

Wildavsky, Aaron. 1979. *Speaking Truth to Power: The Art and Craft of Policy Analysis.* Boston, MA: Little, Brown.

Winston, Clifford. 1998. "U.S. Industry Adjustment to Economic Deregulation." *Journal of Economic Perspectives* 12, no. 3 (Summer): 89–110.

How Effective Is
Policy Analysis?

JOHN A. HIRD

The Wildavsky Forum's invitation to address whether policy analysis is effective is at once provocative and threatening, particularly coming from a premier school of public policy. After all, if policy analysis is ineffective, there isn't much need for public policy schools. In this chapter, I try to address this complex question head-on. I conclude that policy analysis is alive and well, though not in the form its founders intended or that is taught in schools of public policy. Nonetheless, policy schools play a critical role in training policy analysts.

We first need to unpack the concept of policy analysis and what it means to use analysis. The apparently straightforward question of whether policy analysis matters begs at least two additional questions: What is policy analysis? Effective at what? Definitions of policy analysis vary widely. At its broadest and in its most common use, policy analysis is conceived as any form of policy-relevant research. For example, scientific investigations into the causes or consequences of climate change represent a broad form of policy analysis, as does virtually all social science research. Indeed, given the breadth of current and emerging public policy issues, it is challenging to find research without some potential policy relevance. A narrower conception of policy analysis is the one taught in policy schools throughout the United States and internationally, as exemplified by Eugene Bardach's well-known "eightfold path" of policy analysis. This includes a specific series of analytic interrogations, requiring the policy analyst to address problem definition, criteria, analysis of all relevant alternatives, legal, organizational, and political concerns, and an actionable policy recommendation. As it turns out, the effectiveness of policy analysis hinges importantly on these definitions.

WHAT DO WE KNOW ABOUT THE USE OF RESEARCH IN POLICY MAKING?

Policy analysis broadly defined—*any* policy-relevant research and analysis—clearly affects policy making in ways subtle and direct.[1] Two recent examples illustrate how research changed the policy debate in their respective fields, one through agenda setting and the second through direct impact on the policy debate. Both involve important issues, and many other examples exist.

The first involves agenda setting on the issue of inequality. While there are many important contributors to this debate, the social science research that has had perhaps the most significant impact over time is that by the economists Emmanual Saez and Thomas Piketty. Beyond the importance of the topic, their work is influential for several reasons: it is first-rate social science; it covers long periods of time, identifying dramatic swings over the past hundred years; it focuses attention not just on the top "one percent" of the income distribution, but isolated the top 0.1

percent and even the top 0.01 percent; it compares inequality trends with other industrialized nations; and it has shown the important relationship between tax policy and income distribution.[2] There is as a result no serious debate about the changes in income distribution, only what if any policy interventions should follow.[3] Setting the terms of debate and bounding policy options are critical contributions of social science. Social science is capable of contributing important insights into the causes of inequality, as well as the political, economic, and social consequences of various possible policy interventions.

Another example involves a recent finding by my colleagues at UMass-Amherst. In a graduate econometrics class that starts with students replicating previously published studies, one graduate student found that an important study underpinning the belief that high levels of government debt slow national economic growth—by the Harvard economists Carmen Reinhart and Kenneth Rogoff (2010)—had factual and interpretive mistakes that rendered the study's analysis erroneous and, therefore, the policy implications suspect (Herndon, Ash, and Pollin 2013. This change in the interpretation of one key study altered the political argument over austerity policy in important ways, which led to worldwide press coverage. The International Monetary Fund subsequently refuted the Reinhart and Rogoff conclusions as well (Pescatori, Sandri, and Simon 2014) The point is both that social science often undergirds policy positions (the Reinhart and Rogoff study) and that challenges to the veracity of a study can upset the implied policy claims and arguments for the policy recommendations that follow.

There are many examples of social science's impact on policy making—at least in the broader sense of what "impact" means—ranging from the effects of pre-kindergarten programs on student success to anthropologists (controversially) assisting the U.S. military in Afghanistan. (Hernández 2014; Kristoff 2014; Star 2011) To take another example, a recent scientific review by a four-member review panel on wolf protection for the U.S. Fish and Wildlife Service rejected the science underpinning relaxing hunting restrictions, and "the verdict is widely seen as a game changer" (Morell 2014: 719). Courts, too, are frequently the sites of contested social science research. A recent example involves attempts—including "a concerted and expensive effort by conservatives to sponsor research by sympathetic scholars"— to bring to federal court social science study conclusions that show that "children of same-sex couples do not fare as well as those raised by married heterosexuals" (Eckholm 2014: 16) The point is that the findings of social science research are frequently the locus of contestation for important public policy debates. However, while there is copious anecdotal evidence, there is little systematic investigation of how research and analysis are used in policy making.

WHAT DOES IT MEAN TO "USE" RESEARCH?

The social sciences emerged in organized disciplines in the late nineteenth century born of reform impulses, though they quickly embraced scientific objectivity and value neutrality. From this social science orientation, policy analysis emerged with the intention of helping policy makers solve public problems. As Radin (2013: 126) states, "During the early years of the policy analysis field, there seemed to be an implicit acceptance that analysts would be governed by the norms of neutrality and objectivity that were embedded in their culture." At that time, in addition to helping solve pervasive public problems, analysis was expected to drive decision making. These high-minded origins helped define how policy analysis was conceived and how it continues to be taught in schools of public policy to this day.

Part of the challenge for policy analysis is its founding in an era when analysis was seen to trump politics, when policy makers were thought to be on the verge of "fine tuning" the economy, meeting the challenge of communism around the world, and winning the war on poverty. Believing that knowledge can and should inform power, particularly at the national level in the early 1960s when confidence in government was high, social science was thought to offer special insight into successful policy making, leading to social experiments, the establishment of policy schools, new analytic shops in federal agencies, and the placement of social scientists in high-level policy positions. It also coincided with sometimes naive understandings of how knowledge could be "transferred" to policy makers, that is, by "speaking truth to power."[4] As Carol Weiss (2009: ix) puts it, "Social scientists have been hopeful that once accurate research tools and statistics are available, policymakers will pay attention to them and do something different from what they were apt to do in the absence of such knowledge."

A natural extension of this optimism was the emergence of scholarly research seeking clear and observable influences of research on policy making, a task that turned up limited evidence. Early evaluations of some Great Society social programs found unexpectedly weak or nonexistent impacts. Research on whether social science was utilized noted that "use" is an ambiguous concept. Scholars came to accept that research and policy analysis were not used in the traditional, instrumental way as originally conceived: to directly influence public policy decisions. Instead, as Weiss (1979) observed, research and analysis have many more potential uses than those identified in the early days of policy analysis, including some regarded as anathema to the policy analysis enterprise. These include Weiss's political model, where analysis is used to bolster preexisting policy preferences, or her tactical model, where research is used as evidence that an agency is "doing something" about the problem. Indeed, scholars now acknowledge that research is more likely to be used to justify policy decisions than to persuade policy makers. A National Research Council (NRC 2012: 35) report summarizes the challenges: "Scholarship on what happens at the interface of science and policy has to contend with two phenomena—policymaking and use—that are particularly difficult to define."

For decades scholars sought to identify the conditions under which research, broadly defined, influences policy decisions.[5] There are, however, two principal analytic challenges. The first is that the relationship between research and policy-making outcomes is circuitous at best. Even policy makers frequently have trouble pinpointing when, exactly, they are either making decisions or using research. There are copious congressional hearings, meetings, memos, conversations, and other inputs that precede a policy decision, yet how if at all they factor into policy decisions is practically indecipherable. According to the same NRC report, "Policy arguments generally constitute a package of considerations backed by reasons presented to persuade particular audiences of the validity of and need for a given action.... Obviously, it is a complex undertaking to sort out how the multiple characteristics of a policy argument function together to yield a coherent, valid, and persuasive argument" (2012: 55).

The second difficulty in untangling research utilization is that policy makers rarely provide the public with specific justifications for selecting a particular policy. Political solutions rely on participants agreeing on policy solutions, often for different reasons. The challenges of assembling a political coalition in support of a policy proposal are difficult enough without also stipulating that participants must agree on *why* they support the policy. Therefore, ascribing one rationale for choosing a policy proposal can threaten its passage, since other supporters often have different rationales. (More on this later.)

Contemporary research on the use of science in policy making adopts a more nuanced approach, recognizing that policy makers use research in various ways and under varying conditions. The expanded conception of use coincided with recognition that policy makers rarely altered their positions on the basis of new science. Weiss aptly summarized prior research:

> Public officials use research more widely than previous laments on the subject have suggested. But they do not often use it by considering the findings of one study in the context of a specific pending decision and adopting the course of action recommended by (or derived directly from) the research. That kind of instrumental 'utilization' is what many observers have expected and looked for in vain. (1980: 396–97)

A study of the influence of think tanks—institutions designed to influence policy makers—corroborates Weiss's observations: "It is rare to find uncontested examples of a one-to-one correspondence between a think tank report and a policy adopted subsequently by government" (Stone and Denham 2004: 11).

While a full review of the literature on knowledge utilization is beyond the scope of this chapter, numerous studies document the various ways research is drawn upon in policy-making debates. Individual case studies identify subtle research uses, the best of which (e.g., George 1993; Henig 2008) point to the many ways research is used and manipulated for political effect. One scholar concludes that "by all accounts, the most common form of legislative use is support for preexisting positions" (Weiss 1989: 425). Even international technical standard setting, a process seemingly susceptible to expert advice, is anything but: "Standards do not embody some objective truth or undisputed scientific wisdom professed by experts.... The essence of global rulemaking ... is political" (Büthe and Mattli 2011: 11–12). Surveys of senior national security policy makers indicate that while research is utilized, "our results call into question the direct relevance to policymakers of the most scientific approaches to international relations. And they at best seriously qualify the 'trickle down' theory that basic social science research eventually influences policymakers" (Avey and Desch 2014).[6] In contrast, a study of scientists in the European Commission's expert committees found that instrumental use of knowledge (to increase problem-solving capabilities) was prominent (Rimkutè and Haverland 2014), though one might expect scientists to be more sanguine about the use of science in policy making.

More recent summaries of research utilization in policy making draw similar conclusions. The 2012 NRC report states, "Despite their considerable value in other respects, studies of knowledge utilization have not advanced understanding of the use of evidence in the policy process much beyond the decades-old [1978] National Research Council report" (51). The 2012 NRC review reaches a similar conclusion: "We lack systematic evidence as to whether these steps [to connect scientific knowledge and policy] are having the results their sponsors hope for" (31). Following a thorough review of the literature, it notes that "the focus on operationalizing 'use' has not provided an adequate understanding of what happens between science and policy in policy making" (31) and concludes that "the scholarship on use to date is inadequate." (33). While there are many anecdotes of how research is used (or abused) in policy making, there is little systematic examination of the nature and scope of the use of research, and accordingly there are few broad conclusions about if and how research—using this broad definition of policy analysis—can be most effectively connected with policy making.

A NEWER APPROACH TO UNDERSTANDING RESEARCH USE IN POLICY MAKING

Recent work highlights a promising avenue to understanding how research informs regulatory policy making across a wide range of policy arenas, one that avoids some of the challenges affecting previous analyses. (The work is supported by NSF award SciSIP-1360104; Desmarais and Hird 2014; Costa, Desmarais, and Hird 2016) Before detailing this work and its relationship to the effectiveness of policy analysis, some background on the regulatory process and policy analysis is warranted.

One scholarly treatise on regulation notes that "rulemaking is the single most important function performed by agencies of government" (Kerwin and Furlong 2011: xi). U.S. regulations carry the force of law since Congress delegates to regulatory agencies the authority to act on its behalf. While Congress sets the broad outlines of regulatory agency authority, members of Congress recognize that regulatory agencies hold expertise they lack, for example, determining the precise amount of allowable ozone in the atmosphere, whether a new drug or chemical is sufficiently safe, or whether automobile manufacturers should be required to adopt specific new safety features. Examples of federal agencies with broad regulatory powers include the Food and Drug Administration, the National Highway Traffic Safety Administration, the Internal Revenue Service, the Federal Reserve Bank, the Federal Communications Commission, and the Environmental Protection Agency, among dozens of others.

Yet Congress does not simply allow regulatory agencies to issue any regulations they choose. Bound by the Administrative Procedures Act of 1946, regulatory agencies are required to follow specific procedures and solicit and respond to public comments before issuing a regulation.[7] If an agency has the authority to issue a rule, it prepares a proposed regulation, along with a regulatory impact analysis (RIA) that provides a rationale and justification for the regulatory choice, which is then published in the *Federal Register.* These proposed regulations are examined by outside parties (interest groups and lobbyists, the general public, and other agencies) and comments are solicited—at one time provided in written submissions held in vast dockets at regulatory agencies and now online. Agencies must then respond to substantive challenges to potential regulatory impacts. Once this formal comment period has passed, normally within sixty to ninety days, the agency may promulgate the final regulation. Court challenges or new legislation can and do alter these outcomes.

While scholars disagree about the importance of the public comments, there is widespread agreement that the prior review by the Office of Information and Regulatory Affairs (OIRA) in the Office of Management and Budget is consequential. Some view its impacts as more benign and informational (e.g., Sunstein 2013) than others (e.g., Coalition for Sensible Safeguards 2013), but few doubt OIRA's impact on the regulatory process. Much of the controversy stems from various interpretations of the usefulness and political consequences of the required RIA. Some view RIAs as mechanisms to delay needed regulations, others view them as inherently anti-regulation because of their association with benefit-cost analysis, and still others view them as a useful balancing of the benefits and costs of proposed regulations.

Mandated regulatory review in the executive branch began in 1981 with President Reagan's Executive Order 12291 and has continued through Democratic and Republican administrations ever since. While the particulars have varied, the basic emphasis on benefit-cost analysis (BCA) to measure the proposed regulation's impacts has been consistent.[8] Essentially, BCA estimates whether the dollar value of the gains to anyone in the society from a policy change exceeds the dollar value of the losses caused by it. When economic gains exceed losses, it is possible to redistribute resources such that the winners *can* compensate the losers and still have a surplus; it is akin to asking whether the policy change makes the total economic pie larger or smaller. For example, a regulation to require that refrigerators be made more energy-efficient would consider whether the aggregate benefits from the electricity saved would exceed the additional manufacturing, distribution, and other costs. If so, *and if winners costlessly compensate losers,* then everyone is made better off. RIAs, a form of policy analysis, are required for all consequential regulations as part of the rule-making process.

We utilize information gleaned from these RIAs—in particular, their invocation of scholarly research to support regulatory choices—to understand how agencies justify their policy selection.[9] RIAs are particularly good instruments for understanding research use because they (1) cover a wide range of policy areas, (2) cover a broad time period (from 1981 through the present), (3) provide a written rationale for the rule-making selection, and (4) have the opportunity to reference research, arguments, and data

from outside sources. RIAs are required to specify the anticipated benefits and costs of proposed regulations, identify and
analyze all relevant alternatives, and justify the choice of the
regulatory approach. They also play a crucial role because political support for agency decisions rests on the legitimacy and
transparency of public justifications. In practice, RIAs serve as a
justification for the agency's proposed regulatory policy, and
agencies have considerable latitude in choosing if and how to
invoke research to support their policy conclusions. As one study
notes, "RIA is a particularly fascinating case for the analysis of
the role of knowledge in policy-making because it has quasi-sci-
entific ambition, but also takes place at the heart of government
where political decisions are transformed into laws, regulations,
and other policy instruments" (Hertin et al. 2009: 413).

In addition to formal requirements, policy makers are motivated in other ways to use research in rulemaking. Even if policy makers have a predetermined policy choice, they are
accountable for that choice and therefore want the best possible
information regarding the policy's impacts (Lupia and McCubbins 1994). This motivation may emerge from wishing to serve
the public interest most effectively or, alternatively, to provide
political cover should the impacts be worse than anticipated.
Our research project does not distinguish different types of use.
Note that "use" is employed in its broadest sense: agencies
invoke scientific research to bolster their rule-making argument. The principal limitation of this approach is that without
further inquiry, we cannot know how agencies use research. It
could be that science is deployed as ex-post justification for prior
policy decisions, tactically to avoid future lawsuits, to inform
decision making, or any number of other purposes. Nonetheless,
some regulatory agencies choose to invoke science in justifying

their rules while others do not, suggesting that science plays one or more particular roles in agency rule making, roles that vary across agencies and over time. Furthermore, research by Claudio Radaelli and Clare Dunlop (2015) has shown that the vast majority of European RIAs do not cite scientific publications; thus future research is needed to uncover why there are large differences in the use of science across U.S. regulatory agencies as well as cross-nationally.

Our preliminary research investigated the frequency and type of research cited by regulatory agencies in 104 major federal regulations between 2008 and 2012, each of which is accompanied by an RIA. The mean number of citations to scholarly publications[10] in each RIA was 13.25, for 1,378 total citations. This rich data source, of all scientific citations in RIAs, permits large-N, cross-agency, intertemporal analyses that cover disparate policy areas. We compare the citation patterns in RIAs to understand the volume and nature of research underpinning regulatory policy making. Specifically, we examine the degree to which RIAs invoke science to justify new regulations. Executive Order 12866, issued by President Clinton in 1993 and still largely the basis of regulatory analysis, requires that each agency "base its decisions on the best reasonably obtainable scientific, technical, economic, and other information concerning the need for, and consequences of, the intended regulation" (Federal Register 1993: 1(b) (7)). While agencies are not required to cite scientific literature in support of their policies, we find that many (though not all) do. Mean citation rates by agency varied widely, from 32.4 cites per RIA at the Environmental Protection Agency (EPA) to 0.43 per RIA by the Department of Interior (and zero at others). Explaining the considerable variation across agencies is a future project. Further details can be found in Desmarais and Hird (2014); all figures below are drawn from this article. This study is the first to examine rule-making citation patterns systematically to identify how and when science is used to support policy making.

We examined various facets of the RIA citations, including the subjects and journals most frequently cited. Figure 1 shows that economics journals are most widely cited, given this set of categories.[11] Among the social sciences, economics is clearly the most widely cited subject. The lower half of figure 1 shows the citations by journal for journals with at least ten citations, with environmental journals most prominently represented. Again, economics journals are the most prominent in the social sciences; the *Journal of Policy Analysis and Management* is the only public policy journal cited in those RIAs this widely.

Another question we addressed is whether better science is more likely to be cited by regulatory policy makers. If policy makers merely seek studies that support their preexisting policy conclusions, then we would not necessarily expect reference to top scientific journals. While this is a larger question requiring more complete analysis, we first analyze whether a journal's impact factor is associated with a higher number of citations by regulatory agencies for each subject category with at least twenty-five journals cited in our sample of RIAs; these include economics, environmental science, and public health. Analytic details can be found in Desmarais and Hird (2014). As reported in figure 2, there is a clear positive association between a journal's impact factor and the predicted number of citations to it. Therefore, regulatory agencies appear to cite research from higher-impact journals more than others in the same subject domain, suggesting that better science matters to regulatory policy makers. Further research is required to more fully test this claim.[12]

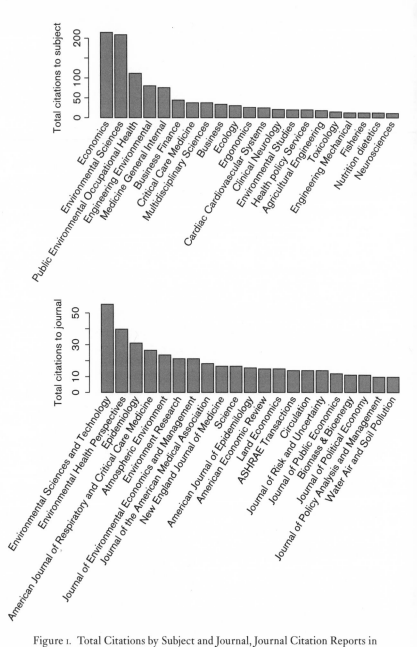

Figure 1. Total Citations by Subject and Journal, Journal Citation Reports in WoS. Reprinted from Desmarais and Hird 2014 with permission from John Wiley & Sons Ltd.

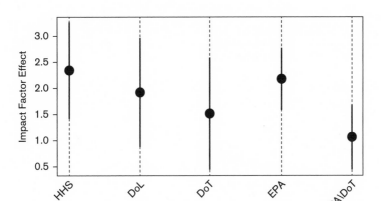

Figure 2. Higher-Impact Journals Cited More than Others. Reprinted from Desmarais and Hird 2014 with permission from John Wiley & Sons Ltd.

Figure 3 illustrates the magnitude of the impact factor's effect across five agencies with more than fifty citations of scholarly publications across our sample. This cross-agency analysis is a check on whether one agency, for example, EPA, is driving the effects of impact factors. We find that journal impact factors are positively related to citation rates in each agency, and that the size of the effect is moderately consistent across agencies. Thus these preliminary analyses suggest that regulators in several agencies are more likely to cite science in journals with greater impact factors, a proxy for better science. Thus if regulators are simply choosing science that bolsters preexisting policy positions, they are not doing so by randomly choosing any science but instead articles in more reputable journals.

While there are many possible future refinements and extensions of this work, the preliminary results indicate that a broad range of agencies choose to invoke scientific research to justify their regulatory decisions.[13] Further, the strong association

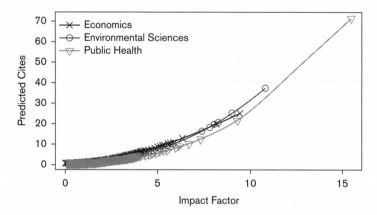

Figure 3. Effect of Impact Factor on the Rate at Which Journals Are Cited in RIAs. Reprinted from Desmarais and Hird 2014 with permission from John Wiley & Sons Ltd.

between a journal's impact factor and its citation in regulatory impact analyses suggests that regulators select citations to articles in more prominent journals, an initial proxy for invoking higher-quality research. Finally, the wide variation in citation patterns across agencies suggests that citations are not simply window dressing—otherwise every agency would use them—though fuller explanations of why some agencies cite research extensively while others do not must await further research.

CLASSICAL POLICY ANALYSIS: A NARROWER INTERPRETATION

The evidence and analysis above illustrates that research is utilized in policymaking, however unclear the motivations or mechanisms remain. Thus, in the broad sense of policy analysis, use is apparent and documented through anecdotes, careful case studies, and systematic analysis. However, when we turn attention to a more focused view of policy analysis, the form that is taught in policy schools throughout the United States and much of the world, the story changes.

There is widespread agreement, at least in the scholarly community, about various elements that constitute a narrower, what I will call the "classical," view of policy analysis. From the earliest days when policy analysis was viewed in purely technical terms (Stokey and Zeckhauser 1978) to broader and more contemporary renderings (Bardach 2012; Weimer and Vining 2005), there are several widely shared principles of policy analysis: it addresses a public problem for a client,[14] develops appropriate criteria, considers all relevant alternatives to address the problem, analyzes the societal implications for each, and furnishes a recommendation that includes considerations of implementation. Weimer and Vining (2005) contrast policy analysis with social science, issue advocacy, policy research, planning, public administration, and journalism. Policy analysis differs from social science research in important ways; the latter does not involve clients, time pressures, or even necessarily policy variables.[15] Beryl Radin (2013: 127) writes, "The attributes associated with the task of policy analysis include problem definition, definition of goals, information collection, choosing and applying analytical techniques, devising options or alternatives, and making recommendations." Furthermore, these elements of policy analysis are taught in virtually all schools of public policy, as well as in cognate degree programs such as public affairs, public policy and administration, and public administration. While policy analysis is widely recognized to be more craft than science, its contours are clear and have been over the past forty years.[16] Thus the conception of classical policy analysis is well understood and widely taught in the United States and abroad.

It is worth distinguishing here not only between the broad interpretation of policy analysis and classical policy analysis but also between the individuals who conduct each of them.[17] Policy researchers—think of academics and scholars at leading think tanks—are distinguished by directing their research to the scholarly community rather than a specific client, a lengthier time frame to conduct the analysis, an emphasis on originality and analytic rigor, and valuing contributions to knowledge. Policy analysts, in contrast, work for a specific client(s); work under sometimes significant time constraints; are normative in orientation in recommending specific actions; must address political, organizational, legal, and other considerations in making recommendations; and value relevance and impact. Finally, policy analysts are trained to serve the somewhat ambiguous concept of the public interest, to promote policies that serve society's best interests. Policy researchers, in contrast, seek to contribute to knowledge and understanding rather than to promote specific policies. Thus not only are the broad and classical versions of policy analysis differentiated, but the people who conduct them are different by temperament, skill set, and occupation.

Since the 1960s, when policy analysis became a known quantity, policy schools have sprouted throughout the United States and increasingly abroad, producing thousands of policy analysts each year.[18] As Radin (2013) notes, their career paths and other characteristics have changed significantly, yet their numbers have increased and their impact has spread throughout all levels of government as well as the voluntary, nonprofit, and private sectors. There are significant changes in the nature and volume of policy analysis over time, including the diffusion of analysis outside government, among advocates, internationally, and throughout agencies rather than "policy shops" at the top of organizational hierarchies. Clients typically are not individual officials but collective bodies. One would expect that if all master of public policy students (MPPs) are trained to conduct classical policy analyses and if policy schools are graduating an increasing number of MPPs who occupy various policy-related positions, including those in the federal government, we would see copious production of classical policy analyses. But, surprisingly, we do not.

WHERE ARE THE CLASSICAL POLICY ANALYSES?

Ironically, there is little evidence of written classical policy analysis, at least at the level that Weimer and Vining or Bardach would conceive of it: client-directed analysis identifying a public problem, comprehensively assessing pros and cons of numerous alternatives, and delivering a policy recommendation accounting for political and organizational factors as well as implementation.[19] There are copious opinions, position papers, budget analyses, testimonies, white papers, memos, and reports but little in the way of classical policy analyses. Establishing the negative—that few policy analyses exist—is challenging, so I offer two examples where we would expect to find frequent use of policy analyses yet find otherwise.[20]

The first example involves the use of policy analysis in state legislatures, where I studied nonpartisan policy research organizations in all fifty states as well as more detailed investigations into a third of them (Hird 2005). Not every state—including my current home state of Massachusetts—has such an organization; the fact that state legislatures choose to establish such organizations implies an institutional interest in unbiased or at least nonpartisan research. Nonetheless, while there are some innovative and successful organizations, for the most part state nonpartisan research organizations were involved in providing information with relatively little analysis. These organizations contribute important information and some short-term analyses but rarely anything even resembling broad policy analysis, much less classical policy analysis. Further, they are not seen as particularly influential, at least in the traditional sense of changing policy outcomes. "Policy analysis in state legislatures appears to fit well the assertion that policy analysis should be, as contemporary understandings suggest, 'more a tool of the democratic process than the problem-solving process" (Shulock 1999: 227); the corollary is that "the empirical reality fits rather poorly the more traditional conception of policy analysis as disinterested analytical problem solving" (Hird 2005: 197–98). Even where state legislatures create policy shops, institutions vital to their inner workings, classical policy analyses are almost nonexistent.[21]

Even the reports of the U.S. Congressional Budget Office (CBO), one of the best known and respected nonpartisan policy research organizations in Washington, present detailed analyses of the implications of various strategies but not recommendations for policy change. Take, for example, their November 2013 report, "Options for Reducing the Deficit: 2014 to 2023." It is a thorough and detailed analysis with scores of policy options, on both the revenue and spending sides, and there is a clear client—Congress—yet it does not include several elements of a classical policy analysis, namely, recommendations and any political or organizational dimensions to potential implementation of these measures. Is it important and relevant analysis? Yes. Is it used in policy making? Most likely. But is it classical policy analysis? No. However, the report is precisely what its client—Congress—wishes.

Similarly, the well-regarded Congressional Research Service (CRS), which produces confidential reports on request from members of Congress, among other products, focuses on analyzing the implications of proposed policies. Its website states, "Staff members analyze current policies and present the impact of proposed policy alternatives." As Radin (2013: 134) writes, "Analysts who work within legislative settings, such as those in the Congressional Research Service, usually try to avoid making recommendations and simply produce analyses that lay out multiple options." Nonpartisan agencies are unlikely to ever produce written policy analyses because, like CBO, the perception of nonpartisanship and unbiased analysis is their raison d'être. As I discuss shortly, issuing policy recommendations may threaten their existence.

A second realm where policy analyses are all but required involves RIAs, referred to earlier. Regulatory agencies are required by executive order to do a number of things, some obvious—"Each agency shall avoid regulations that are inconsistent, incompatible, or duplicative with its other regulations or those of other Federal agencies" (EO 12866, Section 1(b)(10))—and others more controversial, such as numerous entreaties to use economic incentives to achieve results, as well as assessing benefits and costs.[22] The executive order asks agencies to conduct important elements of a policy analysis: identify the problems to be addressed and their significance; consider various alternatives; and assess costs and benefits of all alternatives before reaching (or justifying) a decision that maximizes net benefits (EO 12866, 1993; EO 13563, 2011). Because RIAs should contain many elements of policy analyses and in an organizational environment populated by many policy analysts, we should expect at least minimally competent performance and classical policy analyses.

The evidence shows that mandated requirements do not always lead to enthusiastic agency compliance, however. Several studies have examined the quality of RIAs and generally have found them wanting. RIAs fail to analyze all reasonable alternatives, provide insufficient assessment of costs and benefits, and exhibit wide variation in scope and quality. On a 60-point scale, only twelve of forty-five RIAs reviewed by one study scored higher than 35, with none scoring above 47; the mean score was 27.3 (Ellig and McLaughlin 2012). They are also inattentive to distributional consequences (Robinson, Hammitt, and Zeckhauser 2014). Therefore, in state NPROs, in the federal CBO and CRS, and even where policy analyses are effectively required, as in regulatory impact analyses, we find little to no evidence of classical policy analysis. Perhaps some classical policy analyses exist, though nowhere near the volume implied by the growth in the number of policy analysts or the proliferation of applied social science research.

Table 2 summarizes the conclusions above based on broad and narrow definitions of both policy analysis and use. Policy analysis broadly defined is widely used in informing policy, though it is rare to trace its use to directly driving policy outcomes. In contrast, written classical policy analysis is virtually unknown, though it is likely employed in private personal communication.

WHY SO MUCH ANALYSIS, YET SO LITTLE CLASSICAL POLICY ANALYSIS?

This yields a contemporary paradox: since policy analysts and social science research have proliferated throughout the federal government, why is there so little classical policy analysis? Does that imply that policy analysis is ineffective?

TABLE 2

How Effective Is Policy Analysis?

	Policy Analysis...	
Use...	*Narrowly defined (classical policy analysis)*	*Broadly defined (any policy-relevant analysis)*
Narrowly defined (driving policy)	empty set?	little known use
Broadly defined (informing policy)	personal communications?	often used, though mechanisms unclear

The primary reason we fail to see many classical policy analyses is that policy makers, particularly elected officials, do not want them. Even unelected regulators seem not to embrace classical policy analysis, at least insofar as it is revealed in regulatory impact analyses. Why? Successful politics requires policy makers to form political coalitions to agree on outcomes, not rationales. For example, the broad political acceptance for and increased spending on the federal earned income tax credit (EITC) relies on policy makers on the political left and right supporting the program for different reasons: the Left favors the EITC because it channels income to the working poor; the Right supports the EITC because only wage earners receive benefits. Focusing attention on the rationale as opposed to the policy itself, for example, by conducting a classical policy analysis, would inhibit policy makers from forming political coalitions. It is far easier to reach political agreement on policy outcomes without also agreeing on motivations and rationales.

In addition, elected policy makers do not want classical policy analyses, or even agencies under their institutional control to create policy analyses, because to do so would cede power.

Prime examples are the agencies supporting Congress and state legislatures. They serve at the behest of Congress and state legislatures and exist only if they serve a useful purpose. Thus we can infer from their work products and behavior that what they produce is largely what their institutions wish from them.[23] In virtually all cases, these support agencies do not produce classical policy analyses, and rarely make recommendations, because elected officials are uninterested in ceding control of policy making to policy analysis. Policy makers wish—at best—to know the impacts of potential policies. A classical policy analysis either binds policy makers to the policy recommendation or requires them to provide an alternative rationale for opposing it, neither of which is desirable.

We do not see classical policy analyses because, to the extent such advice is rendered, it is not in writing but likely channeled privately through policy analysts *qua* individuals, that is, through personal contacts. Knowledge utilization scholars attempting to trace the relationship between written policy analysis and policy making are looking in the wrong place; classical policy analysis is more likely to be embedded in people, not formal analyses and reports. Good policy analysts are trained in and embody classical policy analysis: they know what is known and what is knowable (and what is unknowable); they know the relevant criteria; they know the advantages and disadvantages of various policy options; they know their clients' needs; and they are prepared to offer policy recommendations, though orally and privately. Classical policy analysis exists, just not in conventional written reports. The point is that policy analysis—conveyed through people—likely infuses decision making in far more subtle ways than examining whether written policy analyses are produced and used in decision making.

Personal contacts and proximity to power still matter; otherwise, think tanks and other "boundary organizations" would be scattered throughout the country or centered near knowledge-producing institutions such as universities. Instead, even where information transmittal is nearly costless, think tanks congregate in Washington, DC, state capitals, and other sites of political power. Personal contacts and networks are critical to effective policy analysis, research, and influence. Similarly, most policy analysts are located near policy-making centers. Personal contact matters in developing trust between analysts and decision makers and because policy analysis is more likely to be conveyed through networks and repeated personal interactions. As I have noted elsewhere, "It appears that those institutionally focused on affecting policy changes are drawn more to geographic proximity to power than proximity to intellectual producers, to demand more than supply.... The location of think tanks near power suggests that it is far easier to access research at a distance than to influence policy making from afar" (Hird 2009: 526).

Policy makers in Washington, DC, and other centers of large wealthy democracies have significant volumes of analysis at their disposal. Aside from the long-standing formal policy analysis capabilities in federal agencies as well as those supporting Congress (CBO, CRS, GAO, committee staff, etc.), the past several decades have witnessed a veritable explosion in analysis from think tanks, interest groups, news media, and more. If, as Aaron Wildavsky (1979: 9) said, "the purpose of analysis is to connect knowledge with power, not ignorance with weakness," then analysis has been successful. Evidence and analysis still matter to political discourse, though not in the way implied by classical policy analysis. What matters is that policy analysis is

valued by and engages with policy making.[24] Current debates
are framed with at least a patina of research, and arguments are
rendered that rely on research underpinnings, sometimes genuine and sometimes contrived.[25] The key is that public debate
privileges credible research and that credible research can be
publicly and reliably differentiated from shoddy work. It is more
important that policy makers are presented with sufficient evidence and breadth of alternatives to make informed choices than
whether they are presented with classical written policy analyses. We have a healthier democracy when policy makers look
for, or even use as *ex-post* justification, evidence that policies are
likely to work. The polity cannot be healthy if power fails to
seek truth.

Broad forms of policy analysis continue to be used because
policy makers need analysis for instrumental reasons. While
researchers remain uncertain of the conditions under which
broad forms of policy analysis are used, there is little doubt that
it plays a role in policy making, even if that role is to bolster preexisting policy preferences. The fact that policy debates, including legal challenges, continue to hinge on argumentation and
evidence suggests a continuing role for this broad form of policy
analysis.

However, in subjugating politics to rational analysis, classical
policy analysis rendered itself unuseful in practice. Belief that
rational analysis was the missing element in solving major public problems—a view prevalent in the early 1960s, giving rise to
classical policy analysis—implied a shift in power from politics
to analysis. The birth of classical policy analysis recognized the
role of politics in policy making as well as the importance of the
client to whom the analysis is directed, though politics could be

seen as subservient to the analytic process. The belief that the "right" argument based on the best possible analysis would ultimately win the day is woven through classical policy analysis to this day, which naturally included the key step of making policy recommendations, speaking truth to power. Technical solutions rendered by analytically sophisticated and therefore powerful policy analysts were thought to be both valued by policy makers and to drive policy outcomes. This made for an appealing profession for smart, idealistic students who wanted to improve society, though it disregarded the fact that the source and nature of power would remain unchanged.

Ironically, the client orientation of classical policy analysis mitigates its impact, particularly the emphasis on rendering policy recommendations. The client orientation and classical policy analysis are incompatible. The problem with classical policy analysis is not that policy making should be uninformed by analysis but the presumption that policy makers will seek and listen to written policy recommendations. Many policy makers want analysis, but they do not seek public recommendations from their analysts. It is both acceptable and valuable for CBO and other government institutions to render judgments about the implications of various policy proposals, but policy makers are unlikely to employ analysts to make policy recommendations in public. (Lobbyists and interest groups are all too willing to fill that void.) It is not because "truth" doesn't matter but because policy makers are not about to cede power to analysts. The paradox of policy analysis—that so many policy analysts are hired in policy making circles yet we see essentially no classical policy analysis—is that analysis still matters, just not in the way developed through classical policy analysis.

IMPLICATIONS FOR SCIENTISTS AND
"CUSTODIANS OF THE KNOWABLE"

Is the implication that scientists and other knowledge producers should become directly involved in making policy recommendations? Research indicates that while scientists have earned considerable respect from the general public, they do not enjoy the same level of trust (Fiske 2013).[26] Kathleen Hall Jamieson (2013) models the scientific and more generally the knowledge-creating community—scientists, as well as government information producers such as the Bureau of Labor Statistics, CBO, the Census Bureau, and those who generate knowledge, use best available methods, and improve their methods— as "custodians of the knowable." These custodians communicate what is knowable with the best available evidence. This is separate from the imperatives of Jamieson's "journalistic community," where being transparent and policing the community are critical functions. This community needs to be clear to the public about what it is doing and how it is doing it. Both inform the policy-making community. According to Jamieson, if both communities—custodians and journalists—do their jobs well, they can hold the policy-making community accountable for misrepresentations of the knowable.

Scientists and other custodians of the knowable should be clear when they are opining on public policy issues as informed citizens and when they are conveying science-based knowledge relevant to public policy.[27] A collective action problem plagues the enterprise, however. Scientists have personal and institutional incentives to be relevant to contemporary policy issues, yet they can compromise the public's trust in the scientific community by making extrascientific pronouncements. As Weinberg (1972: 216) noted, separating science from trans-science "often requires the kind of selfless honesty which a scientist or engineer with a position or status to maintain finds hard to exercise." Individual incentives (fame, influence) can pull scientists to embellish, mask uncertainties, and provide advice on issues beyond their immediate expertise, all of which can bring attention to the scientist but erode the value of the scientific enterprise. With the proliferation of direct paths to the media and policy worlds, particularly via social media, this is potentially dangerous to science. One scientist, Ken Caldeira of the Carnegie Institute, has noted:

> The issue of going beyond expertise is an important one. There is a disease wherein one develops expertise in one area and then feels free to pontificate on other areas about which one knows nothing. This is an affliction of many senior scientists, common even among Nobel Prize winners, and an affliction to which I have not been immune. If someone is speaking with great confidence while uttering pure hogwash, this does tend to reduce confidence in the utterances of the scientist. So, there is a cost to science and to our personal credibility when scientists make poorly supported assertions in areas outside of their expertise. In any case, scientists should be clear when they are making an assertion that is an empirical fact and when they are simply expressing their values and political opinions. Human beings do have a responsibility to speak out on issues that we feel strongly about. (Quoted in Revkin 2014)

Susan Solomon, former senior scientist at NOAA and heavily involved in two Intergovernmental Panel on Climate Change (IPCC) reports, exemplifies how scientists can maintain scientific integrity, yet still be effective in policy circles:

> When a reporter asked Dr. Solomon to "sum up what kind of urgency this sort of report should convey to policymakers," she

gave the furthest thing from a convenient sound bite. "I can only give you something that's going to disappoint you, sir, and that is that it's my personal scientific approach to say it's not my role to try to communicate what should be done," Dr. Solomon said. "I believe that is a societal choice. I believe science is one input to that choice, and I also believe that science can best serve society by refraining from going beyond its expertise. In my view, that's what the I.P.C.C. also is all about, namely not trying to make policy-prescriptive statements, but policy-relevant statements. (Revkin 2007)

She continued later in the interview, "I take the view that I'll talk about science, but that policy is a collective decision. There are a lot of different ways different people view this. This is reflective of the fact that scientists are human beings like everyone else" (Revkin 2007) As one observer noted, "If scientists do not scrupulously guard a certain minimum of detachment and self-restraint, what do they have to offer that the next man does not? If all questions are political, why not leave them all to politicians?" (Robert L. Bartley, quoted in Weinberg 1972: 220). Scientists can and should involve themselves in the policy-making process, but they should clearly separate their participation *qua* scientist from that *qua* citizen. If science is reduced to just another interest group, it will have lost what makes science special and, because scientists have little funding or constituents to deliver, a particularly weak and ineffective interest group at that. Policy analysts are the appropriate people to fill this gap.

TEACHING POLICY ANALYSIS

Medical schools teach prospective doctors to diagnose and treat illnesses they will encounter in practice. Lawyers are trained to make arguments and write briefs similar to those they will perform in practice. Dentists, landscape designers, artists: all practice in school what they will perform in their careers. However, schools of public policy are instructing students to write classical policy analyses, which they will never produce in practice. Since policy analysis defined broadly still matters in policy making, yet classical policy analysis is imperceptible, this begs the question of whether teaching classical policy analysis in graduate schools of public policy still makes sense.

Classical policy analysis, however absent from actual policy making, remains an important vehicle for teaching policy analysts the connections between their analysis and the policy-making world in which their recommendations would live. Even if it implies more power than analysts will ever have, classical policy analysis teaches that politics, law, implementation, social structures, organizational behavior, and other factors are critical to policy outcomes and must play key roles in thinking through possible ways to address policy problems. Bringing policy ideas to fruition, bridging the worlds of research and policy making, is a critical skill for analysts to develop.

In addition, policy schools are instilling in prospective policy analysts the structure and habits of mind to engage successfully in the policy enterprise.[28] Teaching disciplined thinking for public service is important. Policy analysts not only have a problem-oriented, interdisciplinary approach to policy and the ability to synthesize and bring policy relevance to problems that social scientists are not trained for, but they understand the "rational lunacy of policy-making systems" (Weiss 2009).

In the absence of written classical policy analyses, policy analysts become their human embodiment. Their training will provide a mental picture of how a classical policy analysis *should be performed*. They can derive elements of policy analysis from writing position papers, briefing policy makers, and controlling meetings. They anticipate counterarguments and frame their analyses recognizing alternative options. In short, the mental map of a policy analysis allows good policy analysts not only to be effective in their jobs but also to advance into the public debate the appropriate elements of a policy analysis. Further, the problem orientation of policy analysis focuses at least some attention on social problems, not just political expediency. The role of policy analysts is not merely to translate research for policy makers, but to use creative means to turn available knowledge about the implications of various policy options into actionable policy recommendations appropriate for their clients. This is a subtle skill requiring attention to both political realities and the best available research.

Finally, prospective policy analysts are instructed repeatedly about the importance of their relationship to the client(s), yet far less attention is paid to the other part of the policy analyst's relationship: to the community of knowledge producers. Policy analysts play critical roles as intermediaries between "custodians of the knowable" and policy makers. Their training should include the ability to understand and interpret the academic literature on a topic at a far deeper level than most journalists have the time or, often, the analytic skill set to uncover. Identifying and connecting pertinent knowledge and analysis with policy makers should be a core principle of a public policy education. Policy analysts may offer the central means to provide policy makers with the key elements of classical policy analysis, though not in the way, through written reports, it was originally conceived. Creating a profession for committed, accomplished, and well-trained individuals to participate in the world of public policy may be among the most important contributions of policy analysis education.

NOTES

1. John Maynard Keynes's well-known quote illustrates a view of the subtle, longer-term impacts of ideas: "Practical men who believe themselves to be quite exempt from any intellectual influence, are usually the slaves of some defunct economist. Madmen in authority, who hear voices in the air, are distilling their frenzy from some academic scribbler of a few years back."

2. See, e.g, Alvaredo et al. 2013.

3. Piketty's best-selling *Capital in the Twenty-First Century* (2013) overshadows his substantial earlier contributions to the issue of economic inequality.

4. Aaron Wildavsky, commenting on the title of his book *Speaking Truth to Power,* wrote, "If only we had either!" (1979: 1).

5. The journal *Knowledge: Creation, Diffusion, Utilization* was launched in 1976 to promote and chronicle the research, though it ceased publication in the mid-1990s.

6. At the same time, scholars should not overestimate their potential contributions to public policy. As Stephen Krasner, a Stanford international relations scholar who has also served in the policy world, has said, "I'm extremely skeptical of the notion that there's some repository of wisdom residing in academia, which, if only policymakers paid attention, would provide us with a much more effective foreign policy" (quoted in McMurtrie 2013).

7. Congress's regulatory powers are more than procedural, however. Congress has oversight authority, budget authority, and lawmaking authority that can constrain or enhance agency rule-making powers.

8. RIAs are not synonymous with benefit-cost analyses, however. While RIAs are intended to measure all relevant benefits and costs, they are also required to account for impacts on subpopulations to avoid particularly inequitable outcomes, specify performance objectives, identify alternatives to regulation, and more.

9. We do not claim that RIAs drive policy outcomes in a way intended by classical policy analysis (outlined later in the chapter), but they are at least policy justifications and thus provide the evidentiary underpinnings of policy choice.

10. A "scholarly publication" is one listed in a journal in the Web of Science, common practice in bibliometric work.

11. Other subject categorizations, such as environmental studies, could produce categories with more citations.

12. As noted above, it will require greater analysis to more confidently support this assertion. Of course, a journal's impact factor is imperfectly related to the impact of the article and the author themselves, and impact factors, citation counts, etc., are only partial measures of research quality. We plan additional bibliometric analysis to explore these issues further.

13. In future research, we plan to analyze various network associations (funders, authors, congressional oversight committees, agencies, etc.), as well as the impacts of political controversy, agency culture, and other factors on the use of science in policy making.

14. As one policy scholar put it, "If you do not have a client, you are not doing policy analysis" (Behn 1985: 428).

15. An important distinction between social science and policy research is the latter's inclusion of manipulable policy variables in the analysis.

16. Faculty teach policy analysis in similar ways across professional programs in public policy. We employ similar books, use similar pedagogies (e.g., case studies), teach similar skills (integration of economic, organizational, and political behavior, memo writing, thinking about implementation, etc.), and convey the "art and craft" of policy analysis. Bardach's book is used extensively, as well as Weimer and Vining and others, yet books by Deborah Stone, Munger, Radin, Fischer, and others provide other perspectives on the field and its purpose. Most schools teach the multiple (though not sequential) steps required to conduct a policy analysis, whether three or five or eight steps.

17. This distinction is described thoroughly in Weimer and Vining 2005.

18. Given that there are different definitions of policy analysis, how do we define a policy analyst? I define policy analysts as those individuals capable of performing a classical policy analysis, à la Bardach. At the very minimum, this should include all graduate students completing degrees in public policy and related fields where

one or more courses in policy analysis are taught. Bob Behn (1985: 430) has argued, "To do policy analysis well requires intellectual honesty, political creativity, a respect for a diversity of values, and ability to deflate phoniness, and some scientific rigor." This definition includes more than just graduates of schools of public policy, such as some social scientists who enter the public policy arena, some lawyers with training in research methods, and various others. So defined, significant numbers of people in Washington, DC, and state capitals are policy analysts, whether or not they perform classical policy analyses.

19. In their original book on policy analysis, Weimer and Vining did not include an example, though they thought it important enough to add to subsequent editions. Bardach's classic volume too did not initially include an example, though later editions did. His fourth edition, for example, includes an excerpted RAND study, which he notes was selected for its "thorough and focused analysis as well as its concise presentation" (Bardach 2012: 125).

20. If I am wrong, and there are troves of classical policy analyses generated for policy makers each year that I am unaware of, we could subject them to analyses relating their use to policy making and better understand whether and how they affect policy making.

21. Naturally, exceptions exist, such as the reports of the Little Hoover Commission in California, which develops policy recommendations. However, strong state institutions, such as Kentucky's Long Term Policy Research Center, which produced fine research for the state, have been defunded, in this case in 2010, further eroding policy analysis capacity at the state level.

22. Thus the executive orders are not purely procedural mandates, requiring not only benefit-cost analysis but particular policy mechanisms, such as economic incentives.

23. The defunding and dissolution of the Congressional Office of Technology Assessment is an example of an agency that, for all of its good work and supporters, did not have the support of congressional leaders by 1995.

24. Political polarization exacerbates the problem, for two reasons, one demand side and one supply side. First, polarization inhibits any meaningful search for new or competing ideas. The search for research

and analysis is purely political (Weiss 1979). Each side knows the policies they wish to pursue, and can scour the literature for supporting evidence. Second, on the supply side, "experts" are recognized and employed when they take extreme, partisan views. As one popular book notes, "An expert doesn't so much argue the various sides of an issue as plant his flag firmly on one side. That's because an expert whose argument reeks (sic) of restraint or nuance doesn't get much attention" (Levitt and Dubner 2009: 148). Distinguishing the best possible methods and research findings is crucial in this environment.

25. Some of what passes as research is simply attempts by an interest group to achieve the veneer of scholarly authenticity. For example, the *New York Times* reported on groups with academic-sounding titles like the Employment Policies Institute: "a widely quoted economic research center whose academic reports have repeatedly warned that increasing the minimum wage could be harmful." Yet, while a nonprofit, the group is funded by the restaurant industry, which naturally stands to benefit from keeping the minimum wage low or abolishing it (Lipton 2014: A1).

26. Throughout, my use of the term "scientists" includes all scientists: natural, biological, and social.

27. Scientists play a crucial role in the policy process in elucidating what we know and how we know it; scientists also provide theoretical frames through which policy makers and citizens can make sense of the world. Alvin Weinberg (1972) made an earlier distinction between science and trans-science: "One must establish what the limits of scientific fact really are, where science ends and trans-science begins" (216); "The most science can do is to inject some intellectual discipline into the republic of trans-science; politics in an open society will surely keep it democratic" (222).

28. I recall an ad in the *Economist* for a science writer; it sought to hire a scientist who could write rather than a journalist who knew something about science, and I think they had it right. There is a habit of mind and inquiry that is important to sustain. The ideal policy analyst is described in the title of Alan Blinder's book, *Hard Heads, Soft Hearts,* or President John F. Kennedy's description of himself as an "idealist without illusions" (Dallek 2013). The Goldman School's website tagline—"The Goldman School transforms smart, dedicated,

service-minded women and men into public policy leaders"—has it right. The point is producing people, not reports, to contribute to the public good. This is where the impact of policy analysis is likely to be greatest.

REFERENCES

Alvaredo, Facundo, Anthony B. Atkinson, Thomas Piketty, and Emmanuel Saez. 2013. "The Top 1 Percent in International and Historical Perspective." *Journal of Economic Perspectives* 27, no. 3 (Summer): 3–20.

Avey, Paul C., and Michael C. Desch. 2014. "What Do Policymakers Want from Us? Results of a Survey of Current and Former Senior National Security Decision-Makers." *International Studies Quarterly* 58, no. 4 (December): 227–46.

Bardach, Eugene. 2012. *A Practical Guide for Policy Analysis: The Eightfold Path to More Effective Problem Solving.* 4th ed. Los Angeles, CA: Sage/CQ Press.

Behn, Robert D. 1985. "Policy Analysts, Clients, and Social Scientists." *Journal of Policy Analysis and Management* 4, no. 3 (Spring): 428–32.

Büthe, Tim, and Walter Mattli. 2011. *The New Global Rulers: The Privatization of Regulation in the World Economy.* Princeton, NJ: Princeton University Press.

Cecot, Caroline, Robert Hahn, Andrea Renda, and Lorna Schrefler. 2008. "An Evaluation of the Quality of Impact Assessment in the European Union with Lessons for the US and the EU." *Regulation & Governance* 2: 405–24.

Coalition for Sensible Safeguards. 2013. "Down the Regulatory Rabbit Hole: How Corporate Influence, Judicial Review and a Lack of Transparency Delay Crucial Rules and Harm the Public." June.

Costa, Mia, Bruce A. Desmarais, and John A. Hird. 2016. "Science Use in Regulatory Impact Analysis: The Effects of Political Attention and Controversy." *Review of Policy Research* 33 (3): 251–69.

Dallek, Robert. 2013. *Camelot's Court: Inside the Kennedy White House.* New York: HarperCollins.

Desmarais, Bruce A., and John A. Hird. 2014. "Public Policy's Bibliography: The Use of Research in U.S. Regulatory Impact Analyses." *Regulation & Governance* 8, no. 4 (December): 497–510.

Dunlop, Clare, and Claudio Raedelli. 2015. "Impact Assessment in the European Union: Lessons from a Research Project." *European Journal of Risk Research* 5 (1): 27–34.

Eckholm, Erik. 2014. "Opponents of Same-Sex Marriage Take Bad-for-Children Argument to Court." *New York Times,* February 23, 16–18.

Ellig, Jerry, and Patrick A. McLaughlin. 2012. "The Quality and Use of Regulatory Analysis in 2008." *Risk Analysis* 32 (5): 855–80.

Fiske, Susan. 2013. "Motivated Audiences Beliefs and Attitude Formation." Presentation at the National Academy of Sciences Sackler Colloquia, The Science of Science Communication II. September 23. www.youtube.com/watch?v=Oep_8xERnig&list=PLGJm1x3X QeKoPoWcUGGJzmA_GepNz4Ehf&index=3.

Gawande, Atul. 2013. "Slow Ideas." *New Yorker,* July 29.

George, Alexander L. 1993. *Bridging the Gap: Theory & Practice in Foreign Policy.* Washington, DC: U.S. Institute of Peace Press.

Hernández, Javier C. 2014. "Lessons for de Blasio in New Jersey's Free Pre-K." *New York Times,* January 26.

Herndon, Thomas, Michael Ash, and Robert Pollin. 2013. "Does High Public Debt Consistently Stifle Economic Growth? A Critique of Reinhart and Rogoff." Political Economy Research Institute Working Paper Series #322, April. Accessed at www.peri.umass.edu/fileadmin /pdf/working_papers/working_papers_301–350/WP322.pdf.

Hertin, Julia, Klaus Jacob, Udo Pesch, and Carolina Pacchi. 2009. "The Production and Use of Knowledge in Regulatory Impact Assessment—An Empirical Analysis." *Forest Policy and Economics* 11: 413–21.

Hird, John A. 2009. "The Study and Use of Policy Research in State Legislatures." *International Regional Science Review* 32: 523–35.

———. 2005. *Power, Knowledge, and Politics: Policy Analysis in the States.* Washington, DC: Georgetown University Press.

Hirschman, Albert O. 1977. *The Passions and the Interests: Political Arguments for Capitalism before Its Triumph.* Princeton, NJ: Princeton University Press.

Jamieson, Kathleen Hall. 2013. Sackler Keynote Address, National Academy of Sciences, October 28.

Kahneman, Daniel. 2011. *Thinking Fast and Slow.* New York: Farrar, Straus and Giroux.

Kerwin, Cornelius M., and Scott R. Furlong. 2011. *Rulemaking: How Government Agencies Write Law and Make Policy.* 4th ed. Washington, DC: CQ Press.

Kristof, Nicholas. 2014. "Pre-K: The Great Debate." *New York Times,* January 29.

Levitt, Steven D., and Stephen J. Dubner. 2009. *Freakonomics.* New York: William Morrow.

Lipton, Eric. 2014. "Fight over Wage Illustrates Web of Industry Ties." *New York Times,* February 10, A1.

Lupia, Arthur, and Mathew D. McCubbins. 1994. "Who Controls? Information and the Structure of Legislative Decision Making." *Legislative Studies Quarterly* 19: 361–84.

McMurtrie, Beth. 2013. "Social Scientists Seek New Ways to Influence Public Policy." *Chronicle of Higher Education,* August 30.

Morell, Virginia. 2014. "Science Behind Plan to Ease Wolf Protection Is Flawed, Panel Says." *Science* 343 (February 14): 719.

Nagourney, Adam. 2014. "High-Speed Train in California Is Caught in a Political Storm." *New York Times,* January 7, A9.

National Research Council, Committee on the Use of Social Science Knowledge in Public Policy. 2012. *Using Science as Evidence in Public Policy.* Washington, DC: National Academies Press.

Pescatori, Andrea, Damiano Sandri, and John Simon. 2014. "Debt and Growth: Is There a Magic Threshold?" International Monetary Fund Working Paper, February.

Radin, Beryl A. 2013. *Beyond Machiavelli: Policy Analysis Reaches Midlife.* 2nd ed. Washington, DC: Georgetown University Press.

Reinhart, Carmen, and Kenneth Rogoff. 2009. *This Time Is Different: Eight Centuries of Financial Folly.* Princeton, NJ: Princeton University Press.

———. 2010. "Growth in a Time of Debt." *American Economics Review: Papers & Proceedings* 100: 573–78.

Revkin, Andrew C. 2007. "Melding Science and Diplomacy to Run a Global Climate Review." *New York Times,* February 6.

————. 2014. "Fresh Views on Climate Scientists as Advocates." *New York Times,* January 19.

Rimkutè, Dovilè, and Markus Haverland. 2014. "How Does the European Commission Use Scientific Expertise? Results from a Survey of Scientific Members of the Commission's Expert Committees." *Comparative European Politics* 13 (4): 430–49.

Robinson, Lisa A., James K. Hammitt, and Richard Zeckhauser. 2014. "The Role of Distribution in Regulatory Analysis and Decision Making." Regulatory Policy Program Working Paper RPP–2014–03. Cambridge, MA: Harvard Kennedy School.

Star, Alexander. 2011. "Afghanistan: What the Anthropologists Say." *New York Times Book Review,* November 18.

Stone, Diane, and Andrew Denham, eds. 2004. *Think Tank Traditions: Policy Research and the Politics of Ideas.* Manchester: Manchester University Press.

Stokey, Edith, and Richard Zeckhauser. 1978. *A Primer for Policy Analysis.* New York: Norton.

Stokstad, Erik. 2014. "The Mountaintop Witness." *Science* 343 (February 7): 592–95.

Sunstein, Cass R. 2013. "The Office of Information and Regulatory Affairs: Myths and Realities." *Harvard Law Review* 126: 1838–78.

Weber, Elke U., and Paul C. Stern. 2011. "Public Understanding of Climate Change in the United States." *American Psychologist* (May–June): 315–28.

Weimer, David L., and Aidan R. Vining. 2005. *Policy Analysis: Concepts and Practice.* 4th ed. Upper Saddle River, NJ: Pearson.

Weinberg, Alvin M. 1972. "Science and Trans-Science." *Minerva* 10, no. 2 (April): 209–22.

Weiss, Carol H. 1979. "The Many Meanings of Research Utilization" *Public Administration Review* (September–October): 426–31.

————. 2009. Foreword to Fred Carden, *Knowledge to Policy: Making the Most of Development Research.* Los Angeles, CA: Sage.

Wildavsky, Aaron. 1979. *Speaking Truth to Power: The Art and Craft of Policy Analysis.* Boston, MA: Little, Brown.

CHAPTER THREE

Can Congress Do Policy Analysis?

*The Politics of Problem Solving
on Capitol Hill*

ERIC M. PATASHNIK AND JUSTIN PECK

Each year, scores of well-trained graduates of the nation's public policy schools go to Capitol Hill. Many take jobs with congressional committees or legislative support agencies such as the Government Accountability Office (GAO), the Congressional Research Service (CRS), and the Congressional Budget Office (CBO). They seek to punch a ticket and build their résumés, but many also believe that policy analysis will improve legislative outcomes. Is their faith justified? Does policy analysis happen in Congress, or is it the exclusive province of executive agencies and think tanks? If Congress does engage in policy analysis, can it do so successfully?

An earlier version of this chapter was presented at Representation & Governance: A Conference in Honor of David Mayhew, Yale University, May 29–30, 2013. We thank Richard Bensel, John Ellwood, Alan Gerber, Beryl Radin, Jesse Rothstein, Eric Schickler, Ray Scheppach, Colleen Shogan, Stephen Skowronek, and Craig Volden for helpful comments. All errors of fact or interpretation are our own.

The title of Charles O. Jones's penetrating 1976 essay expresses the dominant view among political scientists: "Why Congress Can't Do Policy Analysis (or words to that effect)." Congress is not an institution "well-structured to conduct policy analysis," Jones (1976: 253) argues, because it is too political a body to bring systematic, unbiased evidence to bear on policy decisions. Congress is a *representative* assembly, not a research bureau. Its internal organization is inconsistent with analytic perceptions and definitions of policy issues (Polsby 1969). Members of Congress are parochial; geographical representation and single-member districts compel lawmakers to respond to local pressures and undermine the incentive to legislate in the national interest (but see Lee 2005). Congress also caters to the demands of interest groups and regularly makes economic decisions that policy analysts find indefensible on efficiency grounds (VanDoren 1989). Unsurprisingly, empirical studies on the instrumental use of policy analysis in Congress have uniformly found that policy analysis reports have little independent impact on legislative behavior and decision making (Shulock 1999; Whiteman 1985).

Yet negative assessments of Congress's capacity for policy analysis cut much too deeply. First, they set unrealistic performance standards for Congress that ignore the constraints of democracy, the complex political context in which Congress operates, and the large variety of ways (both direct and indirect) that policy analysis can contribute to problem solving. Many critics evaluate Congress's performance against the benchmark of a hyper-rational, apolitical model of policy analysis that does not reflect how policy analysis is taught in public policy schools, or, for that matter, practiced in executive agencies (Meltsner 1976). While policy analysis does involve intellectual work and a reasoned search for solutions that further the public interest, it is also a "social and political activity" (Bardach 2009: xv). The purpose of policy analysis is neither to generate knowledge for the academic disciplines nor to prescribe general government decisions but rather to provide targeted decision-making advice to particular organizational clients, which invariably have projects and agendas (Weimer and Vining 1999).[1]

Second, many who assess Congress's performance fail to recognize that Congress is a "they," not an "it" (Shepsle 1992), and that policy analysis in practice is better understood as a collective institutional process rather than as an activity engaged in by a handful of people who see the publication of a report as their primary goal. As a collective process, different congressional actors—including committee staffs, personal staffs, individual members, and party organizations—may contribute pieces at different times during the legislative process. Policy analysis seeks to inform congressional action at different stages of the legislative process, from issue development to oversight of the bureaucracy to program evaluation. Third, many negative assessments overreach by evaluating Congress's performance in a constitutional vacuum, as though Congress is not just one of three national governing institutions (see Mayhew 2009). Congress is the country's *representative* body, and its contributions to problem solving should be viewed in conjunction with what is gained from the larger institutional system of which it is a part.

The most common error that scholars make in assessing Congress's performance as a policy analyst is to construe policy analysis as a simple matter of knowledge acquisition and information processing. In fact, policy analysis is a complex, iterative process comprised of multiple steps or tasks, including defining problems, assembling evidence, constructing alternatives, selecting criteria, projecting outcomes, confronting trade-offs, making decisions, and telling causal stories to an audience (Bardach 2011). No extant study analyzes congressional performance at the task level, even though some of the steps of policy analysis are clearly more compatible with legislative incentives and structures than others. That is the purpose of the present chapter.

The shortcomings we have identified in scholarly treatments of congressional policy analysis often lead observers to overlook the important links between analysis and Congress's institutional responsibilities. Endowed as they are with the constitutional authority to craft legislation relevant to the full range of domestic and global issues, which are growing ever more complex, members of Congress are at a significant disadvantage if they lack the information necessary to understand the consequences of their decisions. Similarly, scholars risk misjudging the capacity of members to address public problems if they fail to understand the strengths and weakness of Congress's capabilities as an analyst. In short, while Section I of the Constitution makes no mention of policy analysis, it is today an unavoidable component of the "legislative powers" (which is not to say that Congress always uses policy analysis effectively).

Policy analysis can also help Congress to satisfy its oversight responsibilities. The large and densely populated administrative apparatus affords modern presidents with significant policy-making powers. Congress, in turn, is frequently charged with ensuring that bureaucrats are efficiently and effectively working to fulfill policy goals. Without the information provided by policy analysis, Congress would find it difficult to engage in oversight. Generally speaking, members are not policy experts. The information provided by analysis, however, allows them to question, oversee, and redirect bureaucrats who have significant "informational" advantages in specific areas of policy. Without analysis, oversight would be a completely empty or symbolic enterprise—which is not to deny that some committee hearings on bureaucratic performance are largely exercises in congressional blame casting (Derthick 1990).

Given the responsibilities assigned to Congress and its structure as a representative body, how well does it utilize policy analysis to solve the public problems it confronts? There is no perfect methodology for assessing how well or poorly Congress carries out the multiple tasks of policy analysis. Our strategy is to draw on three different sources of information to reach conclusions about the institution's central tendencies. The most extensive data source we use is a survey that we conducted in April 2013 of more than 150 Washington area policy analysis professionals who work for universities, think tanks and research organizations, and government agencies. The survey aims to probe a variety of ways and openings through which policy analysis can flow into the legislative process as an input, including during the pre-deliberation stage. (The survey design is described below.)

There are both strengths and limitations to relying on the perspective of this elite sample to evaluate Congress. One major advantage of the survey is that it relies on the opinions of experts who are highly knowledgeable about the concepts, skills, and methodologies of policy analysis, such as cost-benefit analysis. These are technical matters about which even savvy journalists, congressional staff members, and political observers may be poorly informed. Our survey sample is large enough to capture the impressions of the policy analysis expert community while avoiding placing too much weight on the views of a few individuals. Another advantage is that professional policy analysts are a tough-minded group. To the extent such experts perceive Congress's performance as not uniformly negative, it is noteworthy.

The expert survey also has some important limitations, however. First, professional policy analysts (like everyone) have biases. As noted below, approximately 75 percent of our survey respondents profess a liberal bias of one sort or another. While we find no evidence that the ideology of survey respondents correlates with their beliefs about congressional performance, it is important to recognize that the political orientation of our sample is unrepresentative of the American public. Another limitation is that the survey focuses on questions about Congress's overall performance. As a result, the survey results lack the detail and texture of in-depth interviews. We try to overcome this limitation by supplementing our survey findings with the perspectives of current and former congressional policy analysts. In addition to conducting several individual interviews, we held a confidential focus group in Washington, DC, on November 18, 2013, with six senior policy analysts who work for the three key congressional support agencies—the Congressional Budget Office, the Congressional Research Service, and the Government Accountability Office. All the participants have had extensive experience advising Congress across a range of policy areas, including budget, health, and defense. As professional analysts employed by Congress, they can be expected to possess intimate knowledge of how Congress operates and a more sympathetic view of the institution's performance.

Finally, we draw on empirical and theoretical insights from the vast political science literature on Congress, including both classic works on the institution and more focused studies that assess its use of policy analysis on the basis of congressional staff interviews. Taken together, these three data sources give us confidence that we can draw inferences about what policy analysis tasks Congress struggles to perform and what tasks it handles more adroitly. While we do not set out to "save" Congress's reputation, our analysis provides a more balanced and fine-grained view of Congress's strengths and limitations as a problem-solving institution.

The chapter proceeds as follows. The first section defines policy analysis and establishes standards for evaluating Congress's performance. The next section gives an overview of the survey methodology (the text of the survey is presented in Appendix 3–2). The third section—the core of the chapter—evaluates how well Congress performs each of the eight major tasks of policy analysis (Bardach 2011), drawing on all three data sources mentioned above. The concluding section summarizes our main findings and offers some more speculative comments about how secular trends including partisan polarization, the widening of the policy agenda, and the growing complexity of government have interacted with Congress's policy-analytic strengths and weaknesses to affect institutional performance.

WHAT IS POLICY ANALYSIS? RATIONAL, INTERPRETIVE, AND HYBRID MODELS

What is policy analysis? Can Congress do it? What are the standards against which Congress's performance should be assessed?[2] The traditional model of policy analysis defines it as an objective, scientific endeavor in which decision makers set goals and maximize social welfare by using analytic methods and rigorous empirical research to identify the best means to address societal problems (see, e.g., Stokey and Zeckhauser 1978). There are many reasons that the "rational" model of policy analysis is apt to fail on Capitol Hill. Members are occupied with fund-raising and constituent service. They lack the time to think deeply about issues, and instead rely on cues and heuristics to "muddle through" (Lindblom 1959; Schuck 2014). Even more fundamentally, members' main objective is reelection, and political payoffs come from taking pleasing positions and delivering perceptible benefits to constituents, not from crafting efficient policy solutions (Mayhew 1974; but see Arnold 1990). Few legislators, as they pursue their political goals, bother to master the concepts and tools of policy analysis. The typical member finds scientific information "hard to assimilate or relate to policy questions" (Bimber 1991: 601). Legislative structures designed to facilitate reelection—including overlapping committee jurisdictions, the oral tradition, and the reliance on compromise and logrolling—also inhibit the use of analysis (Weiss 1989).

Yet Congress is not impervious to policy analysis. As Allen Schick wrote in 1976, "The argument that Congress will not become a major user of analysis is as untenable as the position that a new analytic era is just over the horizon" (234–36; see also Weiss 1989; Whiteman 1985). Members of Congress can benefit from policy analysis in at least three ways. First, information about problems and solutions helps lawmakers cope with the growing scope and complexity of government and the increasing rate of technological change. Over the decades, Congress has bolstered the informational resources at its disposal as well as its internal capacity for generating and using expertise, including funding professional committee staffs and establishing congressional support agencies (Price 1971; Sundquist 1981; Schickler 2001; Shepsle 1988; Rieselbach 1994). During the 1970s, for example, Congress established the Congressional Budget Office, the Congressional Research Service, and the Office of Technology Assessment (OTA). Second, policy analysis can help members reduce political uncertainty (Krehbiel 1991; Arnold 1990). All else being equal, members would prefer to select policies whose effects are known in advance because it allows them to minimize the potential for surprise or embarrassment. Even if members are not interested in making "good" public policy, the capacity to anticipate allows them to "mak[e] the most of credit-claiming" opportunities and promote their reelection chances (Krehbiel 1991: 62). And third, policy analysis can help Congress maintain its institutional power in the separation of powers system. The rise of the administrative presidency was a major factor in prompting Congress to beef up its analytic capacity. During the 1940s and 1950s, agencies like the Bureau of the Budget provided trusted analysis to both branches. When the presidential branch "captured" these agencies during the Johnson and Nixon administrations, Congress was threatened. Congress responded by creating legislative support agencies to maintain its relative standing in the constitutional order (Moe 1985). While reforms to boost Congress's information-processing capacity are rare (Binder and Quirk 2005), they clearly suggest unwillingness on the part of members to entirely offload the institution's policy analysis responsibilities to the executive.

An alternative, "interpretive" model of policy analysis is more modest in its expectations of Congress—and more nakedly political. According to Nancy Shulock (1999: 229), policy analysis is not a problem-solving, scientific activity but rather an "instrument of democratic process" that is used "(a) as language for framing political discourse; (b) as legitimate rationalization for legislative action where prospective rationality is inhibited by 'garbage can' decision environments; and (c) as a symbol of legitimate decision processes that can increase support for governance processes in a society that values rationality" (see also Stone 2001). Don't be fooled by appearances, Shulock implies.

Members of Congress may *look* like they are carefully weighing options and projecting consequences, but they are just using the positivist forms of policy analysis to create a favorable public impression. While there is no doubt that members of Congress want to look good in the eyes of observers, this view is too cynical. The massive investment in Congress's analytic capacity over the past half century is far more than institutional window dressing.

Ultimately, the rational and interpretive models are best understood as ideal-types. Neither fully captures the complexity of the roles that policy analysts play (or seek to play) in the United States (Radin 2000). Whereas the rational model asks too much of Congress by denying the legitimacy of power and persuasion in policy making, the interpretive model asks too little of the institution by rejecting both the normative, problem-solving focus and the scientific foundation of policy analysis. The challenge is to define policy analysis in a way that reconciles the power of ideas with a sober appraisal of the messy realities of legislative politics.

In our view, policy analysis is best understood as an *amalgam* of intelligence and pragmatic action. Policy analysts seek to develop options that, if adopted, will mitigate problems that people are experiencing in their daily lives. In a democracy, the audience for policy analysis includes "diverse subgroups of politically attuned supporters and opponents of the analyst's work" (Bardach 2011: xv). As such, policy analysis stands between pure planning—in which apolitical, synoptic rationality guides governance—and raw politics—in which the preferences of the powerful dictate policy prescriptions. Aaron Wildavsky developed this more balanced, hybrid model in his classic book *Speaking Truth to Power: The Art and Craft of Policy Analysis:*

> If analysis were purely intellectual, analysts would be everything, or if analysis were purely interactive, analysts would be nothing. Are we faced, then, with a choice between mind without matter or force without foresight? No. Our task is to develop a hybrid, called policy analysis, which uses intellect to help guide rather than replace social interaction. (1979: 124)

Just as the effort to separate politics and administration (Wilson 1887) collapses in skirmishes over policy implementation, so the attempt to quarantine the intellectual work of policy analysis from the politics of democracy crumbles when actors frame problems and advocate solutions. Ideas about how to recast government are the currency of policy analysis, but these ideas are accepted or rejected by actors who have particular projects or interests. Wildavsky (1979) wrote that policy analysis has many faces: among other things, it is *descriptive* (in seeking to explain how a difficulty has come about); *selective* (because oriented to particular people and organizations); *objective* (in aiming to get people to agree on the consequences of options); and *argumentative* (in recognizing that the capacity to convince is essential for political support). Assessments of political feasibility—who supports an idea? what are the obstacles to change? how might these obstacles be overcome?—are integral to policy analysis. The aim of such assessments is not to claim that the feasible is desirable but rather to help make the "desirable do-able" (Wildavsky 1979: 126).

Viewed in this light, the question is not only whether and under what conditions Congress heeds the scientific advice offered by economists (Derthick and Quirk 1985; Schick 1976) but also what Congress contributes to the multifaceted task of problem solving. David Mayhew adopts a similar position:

> To contribute effectively to societal problem solving, [members of Congress] need to be able to help define as "problems" the often

inchoate fancies, preferences or demands of society or its elite sectors. The members need to make such definitions widely known and accepted. They need to frame these problems in ordinary, common sense so as to bring the public along, yet also frame them in a way that adapts to the instrumental-rationality needs of political executives and bureaucrats. They need to merchandise causal stories to a wide audience.... Beyond this, they need to probe evidence reasonably hardheadedly in a search for "solutions." ... It is a tall order, but as a descriptor of congressional activity it does not refer to a null set. (2006: 223)

We use this hybrid model as a more realistic baseline against which to evaluate congressional performance.

SURVEY OF PUBLIC POLICY EXPERTS

We conducted an Internet-based survey of members of the Association for Public Policy Analysis and Management (APPAM), a leading professional association. An invitation to participate in the survey was sent to members who had a mailing address in the greater Washington, DC, area (which includes Maryland and Virginia).[3] In total, approximately 449 people were contacted. The overall response rate was 36 percent (N = 162). The sample included policy analysts from a range of employment backgrounds: 42 percent work in universities or colleges, 36 percent in think tanks or research organizations, 14 percent in the federal executive branch, 8 percent in the federal legislative branch, 8 percent in state or local government, 8 percent work for government contractors, 4 percent work for nonprofit service providers, and 2 percent work for foundations or advocacy organizations. The sample is 58 percent male. Sixty percent of the respondents have a PhD, and 38 percent have a master's or professional degree. Forty-seven percent earned their highest degree in public policy, 21 percent in economics, 14 percent in public administration, 8 percent in political science, and the rest in other fields. The sample also skewed ideologically to the left. On a 7-point scale of political views, 8 percent identified as extremely liberal, 43 percent as liberal, 24 percent as slightly liberal, 15 percent as middle of the road, 4 percent as slightly conservative, 2 percent as conservative, and 0 percent as extremely conservative. Most respondents also report having had direct interactions with members of Congress or congressional staff. Only 20 percent reported never interacting directly with members of Congress or congressional staff. Thirty percent said they had such interactions at least several times a year, 19 percent once a year, and 30 percent on occasion but less than once a year.

While the respondents have no lack of criticisms of the institution's performance, they are not reflexively "anti-Congress." They accept that Congress has a major role to play in national policy making. Only 13 percent said that important domestic policy decisions should be made mostly by the president with some input from Congress. Fifty-nine percent said they thought such decisions should be made by Congress and the president equally, and 26 percent said such decisions should be made mostly by Congress with some input from the president.[4]

Congress and Policy Analysis Tasks

Most studies of Congress and policy analysis have examined whether Congress produces and consumes policy-analytic knowledge (Weiss 1989; Whiteman 1985). This is an essential question, but it is posed at too high a level of abstraction. Policy analysis is a multistep activity combining intelligence and interaction. To separate the pieces of this hybrid model, we use Bardach's well-known conceptual framework (Bardach 2011). Bardach argues that policy analysis consists of eight tasks: (1) defining problems, (2) assembling evidence, (3) constructing alternatives, (4) selecting criteria, (5) projecting outcomes, (6) confronting trade-offs, (7) making decisions, and (8) telling causal stories to an audience. (We treat the tasks as discrete, even though in practice they overlap.) Congress has potential roles to play at each step. We wanted to know how well it performs them.

Defining Problems

The first step of policy analysis is to define the problem. On the surface, Congress looks like a premier problem definer. Countless bills contain proclamations along the lines of "Whereas X is occurring . . . ," where X represents some allegedly serious problem that warrants a legislative solution. Yet while such bold assertions may serve the electoral goals of members, they are often little more than "issue rhetoric" that is too imprecise or emotion-laden to catalyze *pragmatic* problem solving. Instead, to serve as the foundation for policy analysis, a problem must be defined in a way that is "analytically manageable and that makes sense in light of the political and institutional means available for mitigating it" (Bardach 2011: 4).

Survey respondents gave Congress dismal marks as a problem definer. Eighty-one percent of respondents agreed or strongly agreed that Congress is more concerned with "looking good in the eyes of voters than with actually solving problems." Only 3 percent believed that Congress has done a good or better job over the last ten years in "defining problems in ways that are logical and analytically manageable," and 56 percent rated Congress's performance as "poor."[5] What accounts for Congress's poor performance on this step?

Defining problems is a challenging task for a legislature. It requires bringing order to the conflicting demands of voters, experts, and interest groups. It also requires a clear-eyed diagnosis of the source of the difficulties. Even when there is a consensus on the existence of a problem, there may be disagreement about its causes. For example, are the disability rolls expanding because of rising clientele needs or because more people are gaming the system? Are health care costs high because providers charge too much or because consumers do not have enough "skin in the game"? Is unemployment a structural or cyclical problem? Experts themselves may disagree on the answers to these questions; it may be too much to expect a representative assembly to resolve them.

On the basis of interviews with eighty-three individuals serving on the staff of congressional committees and congressional support agencies during the 1980s, Weiss (1989) found that committee staff members reported using analysis primarily to certify positions and influence the priority of proposals on the agenda but tended not to use analysis to reconceptualize problems.[6] Consistent with the findings of Weiss's earlier study, the experts we surveyed overwhelmingly agreed that legislators use evidence to fortify positions they already hold.[7] Eighty-four percent of respondents said they believe that congressional leaders usually know how they wish to address national problems and that they use the recommendations of policy experts to add legitimacy to positions they would have taken anyway. Only 4 percent agreed with the statement that congressional leaders often do not know the best way to address national problems and look to policy experts for guidance on the most effective course of action.

Of course, this begs the question of where members' views come from in the first place (Peterson 1995). Constituency opinion, party positions, and ideology are all potential sources of legislative preferences, but so too is the tenor of the times, to which policy analysis contributes. Policy analysis might still shape legislative problem definitions, but (as we discuss below) it may filter into Congress through more indirect channels at earlier stages of the legislative process (Weiss 1989).

Yet Congress does possess some institutional capacities as a problem definer, especially when its role is evaluated in the context of a separation of powers system. While Congress lacks the executive's ability to frame problems in analytically crisp ways, its openness to outside pressures and demands arguably makes a contribution to the American political system's capacity to address a changing menu of topics over time. About 4 in 10 experts (37 percent) surveyed rated Congress's performance good or better in bringing attention to new issues.

Because developing effective problem definitions is challenging, many experts recommend an iterative process in which understandings of a problem are subject to revision and refinement (Bardach 2011). When confronting complex problems, trial-and-error learning is a defensible approach. By its nature, legislative coalition building is an iterative process in which bill sponsors often modify their initial assumptions in response to input from colleagues whose support they hope to win (Schick 1976). As one analyst we interviewed stated, "Making policy adjustments for political reasons that moves toward a second best solution is often the best way to proceed as it creates more ownership over the final bill. This can be critical as you often need to make technical corrections [after policy enactment]."

Indeed, the process of trial-and-error learning does not end when a bill becomes a law. As E. Scott Adler and John D. Wilkerson observe in their recent book, *Congress and the Politics of Problem Solving* (2012), there has been a significant rise in "temporary" legislation since World War II. While there are many explanations for this trend, including conflict between Congress and the executive, Adler and Wilkerson argue that the increasing reliance on short-term authorizations reflects Congress's desire to preserve the flexibility to update a preexisting policy in light of new information and changing conditions.

Yet congressional learning about problems takes place in a political context shaped by the policy feedback from past legislative activity (Pierson 1993). Whether short-term or permanent, statutes carry the force of law, and laws generate reactions (stop! continue! do more!) among constituencies, to which lawmakers must respond. As government has grown, the policy "space" has become increasingly congested. It is rare today for Congress to legislate in an area not already populated by existing policy commitments (Patashnik 2008; Patashnik and Zelizer 2013). In the contemporary American state, legislators do not define new problems so much as cope with the consequences of earlier "solutions." Consider, for example, Congress's decision to end air traffic furloughs in 2013. That decision reflected Congress's effort to manage the political fallout from budget sequestration, which was itself a (temporary) resolution of the debt-ceiling crisis. In sum, as the complexity of government grows, lawmaking increasingly turns in on itself. Legislators still respond to the demands of constituent groups, but those demands are mediated by the consequences of past decisions. As Wildavsky put it, "Policy becomes more and more its own cause" (1979: 81).

Assembling Evidence

Evidence-based decisions cannot be made unless evidence is assembled. Data must be collected and then turned into information relevant to the policy questions at hand (Bardach 2011). Few members of Congress have the time or desire to keep up with the academic literature, let alone conduct original research studies.

Yet Congress is "awash in policy information" (Bimber 1996: 1). This information is absorbed and packaged not only by congressional committees but also by the staffs of 535 individual member offices. While many of these "congressional enterprises" are not inclined to tap into policy-analytic knowledge, others are highly active and engaged. Staff members at the core of "issue networks" devour policy reports and interact regularly with experts in academia and think tanks (Whiteman 1985; Heclo 1972). Among the most important sources of information for lawmakers are the congressional support agencies—CRS, CBO, GAO, and OTA (before its termination in 1994). While these agencies have suffered significant staff cuts since the 1970s (Drutman and Teles 2015), they continue to issue thousands of detailed reports each year and play a key role in gathering and summarizing evidence and conducing financial analysis for members. Through its analytic support agencies, Congress forges institutional and ideational connections to other sites of the vast U.S. policy analysis enterprise, including the academy, think tanks, and private research organizations like Mathematica and MDRC.

The politics of legislative support agencies highlight the complex relationship between expertise and power in American democracy (Hird 2005; Fisher 2011). To ensure continuing political support, agencies must refrain from criticizing firmly held congressional positions, avoid catching members by surprise, and be attentive to Congress's prerogatives, including its goal of maintaining a balance of power with the executive (Bimber 1996). Members of Congress expect professional, nonpartisan guidance from the support agencies; they also insist on responsiveness to their institutional interests. Support agencies that fail to satisfy the demands of members of Congress, their clients, may be denied the political sustenance required for their survival. In 1995, for example, the Office of Technology Assessment was terminated, among other reasons, because Congress did not view assessments of technology as essential to maintaining a balance of power with the executive (Bimber 1996; Mucciaroni and Quirk 2006). Sometimes support agencies like the CRS and GAO are criticized when they do not follow a model of "neutral competence." Such criticism is unwarranted because *all* policy analysts must satisfy the needs of their organizational clients, and the legislative support agencies are no exception.[8] As one senior analyst who participated in the focus group stated, "I don't like that word [*neutral*] at all. I prefer the word *objective*. Neutral implies that we don't make pronouncements or draw conclusions, but we do—all the time." In a separation of powers system, the requirement that the legislative support agencies be sensitive to Congress's institutional needs—and thus abandon any pretense of "neutrality" on basic constitutional values—is not a weakness but a strength (Fisher 2011).

While the congressional support agencies strive to be nonpartisan, partisan and ideological conflicts over the generation of information can arise when Congress decides whether to request an official government report from an agency. A reporting requirement on a subject of broad legislative interest might seem like a good government issue on which liberals and conservatives would generally agree. As Frances Lee (2009: 121) points out, however, members are well aware that "information is a powerful weapon." A study could favor one side or the other in a partisan debate. Hence congressional votes on information control tend to be either noncontroversial or highly contentious on partisan lines (Lee 2009).

The main way that members learn about policy issues is through interaction with interest groups, not from reading government reports. The conventional wisdom holds that lobbying distorts information-gathering (but see Hall and Deardorff 2006), because narrow special interests are more likely to possess the resources and incentive to convey information to legislators than organizations representing diffuse public interests (Wright 2003). If members simply listen to the advice they get from interest groups, the result may be bad policy. Kevin Esterling (2004) challenges this pessimistic conclusion about the policy consequences of interest group lobbying. Drawing on Gary Becker's model of interest group competition, Esterling argues that advocates of policies that evidence suggests will work well are more likely to invest scarce resources in lobbying efforts than are the groups that would be harmed by the adoption of these policies (Esterling 2004; Becker 1983). In sum, even if members are not motivated to promote good policies, they will do so as a by-product of servicing the organized. Esterling supports his counterintuitive claim through case studies of Congress's use of evidence in the adoption of socially efficient policies, such as the 1990 acid rain emissions trading program.

As Sarah Binder (2006) persuasively argues, however, lawmakers are interested in receiving information not only about the programmatic effects of policy solutions but also about their *political* consequences, such as how support for proposals would affect a member's reelection chances (see also Peterson 1995; Price 1991). There is no reason to think that the information emanating from the political environment will be unbiased or naturally lead members to support Pareto-improving reforms (Binder 2006).[9] Members of Congress are often uninterested in learning information that challenges constituent views on salient issues and are reluctant to incorporate evidence that casts a negative light on programs that benefit well-organized groups. As one focus group participant told us, "Our analytical work has the most influence in micro, technical areas where there are no entrenched views." Members who represent districts with oil companies are unlikely to be interested in evidence about the inefficiency of oil subsidies. The problem of congressional indifference to evidence is arguably most severe when special interests are not geographically concentrated because then there may be no countervailing constituency to their interests. For example, there is compelling evidence that U.S. physicians (prevalent in all jurisdictions) perform many unnecessary medical procedures, but Congress has been hesitant to use this information to strengthen the government's role in reviewing Medicare billings and reducing wasteful health care spending out of fear of antagonizing doctors, providers, and senior citizens across the country (Gerber and Patashnik 2006b). Sometimes clear evidence of a serious national problem exists—but Congress prefers to keep its collective head in the sand.

This mixed assessment of Congress's performance as evidence assembler is reinforced by our survey results and interviews. Sixty-five percent of survey respondents said that Congress has done a poor job over the past ten years in making policy decisions on the basis of objective evidence. To make our inquiry more concrete, we asked survey respondents to reflect on the following scenario: What if a prestigious academic journal publishes a research study that shows that an existing federal transportation program is highly cost-ineffective, meaning that it would be possible to achieve the same transportation benefits at much lower cost or to spend the same amount of money while generating much larger transportation benefits. We asked respondents how likely they thought it was that the chairs of the congressional committees with jurisdiction over the program would become aware of the study. About half of the experts (46 percent) were very or somewhat confident that committee chairs would become aware the study. Respondents who reported having been a legislator or served as a legislative staff member were more confident that the committee chair would learn of the study, but the effect was not statistically significant in all models (All statistical results appear in Appendix 3–1).[10] Just 4 percent of experts were very or somewhat confident that Congress would make a serious attempt to replace the transportation program with a more cost-effective approach, however. We did not pose a follow-up question as to why respondents believed that Congress would fail to act on the findings of the study, but we suspect the most likely answer is that the existing transportation program can be assumed to have vested interests, which Congress will be reluctant to upset.

In sum, the main information problem Congress faces is not the absence of evidence but rather the failure of members to make good use of available information (Quirk 2005). Indeed, only 6 percent of survey respondents said that lack of information is an extremely important reason for Congress's failure as a problem-solving institution. As figure 4 shows, experts were far more likely to name the following factors as extremely impor-

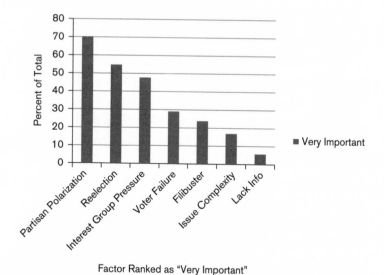

Factor Ranked as "Very Important"

Figure 4. Experts Believe Lack of Information Not the Problem.

tant reasons for Congress's failures to solve problems: partisan polarization (71 percent), lawmakers focused on their own reelection (55 percent), and interest group pressure (48 percent).

Constructing Alternatives

A creative aspect of policy analysis involves the identification of alternative ways to mitigate a problem. Putting multiple policy options on the table ensures that a leader's pet idea doesn't win the day without consideration of other possible solutions. How good is Congress at constructing policy alternatives, and where do members look for inspiration when they seek to develop ways to address an issue on the agenda?

Survey respondents provide a negative assessment of Congress's performance in constructing policy alternatives. Nearly half (47 percent) of the experts surveyed think Congress has done a poor job over the past ten years in developing new policy options for addressing national problems. Only slightly more than 10 percent think that Congress has done a good or mostly good job at this task.

Three developments may explain Congress's poor performance as an option constructor. First, modern presidents have taken on an active role as "legislator in chief," while Congress often assumes a reactive posture in which members respond to executive-initiated agenda items rather than developing an agenda of their own. Indeed, as Cohen (2012) has demonstrated, during the second half of the twentieth century the president's legislative policy agenda became so extensive that legislative activities occupied a central aspect of his political responsibilities. This expansion of the president's legislative responsibilities came at the expense of Congress. As Cohen argues, while Congress "might have been the center of legislative activity" through the Progressive era, presidents "became more central to the legislative process from the second half of the twentieth century onward" (109–10).

Second, committees appear to have lost power at the expense of parties over the past few decades. Policy alternatives need to be grounded in an understanding of the linkages between problems and solutions and the mechanisms by which a particular government intervention can change the behavior of targeted constituencies. The committee process—investigations, bill mark-ups, the questioning of witnesses at hearings—gives members the opportunity to develop such expertise. Andrew Taylor's (2013) recent study of congressional performance suggests, however, that intense partisanship and growing interest group pressure have undermined the quality of committee deliberations. Members come to committee hearings with "fixed preferences and a general unwillingness to change their minds" about how to approach issues (132).

Third, the growth of Big Government, and the generation of vested interest groups that lobby against reform, means that the most important alternative is often current policy. Ironically, members themselves may lack the requisite expertise even to understand the policy status quo. As one focus group participant stated, "Here's a common scenario. Congress passes a vague law, bureaucrats determine how the law is implemented and legislative branch research staff … have to 'explain it back' to members and staff."

In terms of where Congress *does* look for new ideas about how to improve policy, most experts (68 percent) think that Congress never or almost never seeks to learn from the best practices and policy successes of other nations. Less than one percent of experts surveyed said that the typical member's support for a bill would be influenced a lot by whether other nations had adopted similar legislation. When members do look for best practices, they search much closer to home. Forty-eight percent of survey respondents said they believe that Congress seeks to learn from the policy successes of state governments sometimes, and 21 percent believe that Congress seeks to learn from these state-level experiences fairly or very often. This suggests that successful policies may not only transfer across the states (Shipan and Volden 2012) but also spread from one level of government to another. When such policy diffusion occurs, Congress may end up (indirectly) using information that entered the process at an earlier (pre-Congress) stage.

Welfare reform offers a good illustration of how research can shape congressional policy making without leaving a direct imprint on legislative behavior. A number of observers have argued that evaluation research on welfare-to-work experiments helped create the policy conditions that made the Family Support Act of 1988 possible (Haskins 1991). However, while many lawmakers were clearly familiar with these experiments, research was not a decisive factor during either committee mark-up or floor debate (Haskins 1991). Kent Weaver, in his detailed study of the 1996 welfare reform law, similarly finds that lawmakers did not use research in a straightforward, technocratic fashion. Evaluation research did, however, improve the prospects for Republican policy ideas, including deterrence and devolution, by showing that welfare-to-work programs alone would be "inadequate to reduce welfare dependence and recidivism substantially" (Weaver 2000: 168).

In a related vein, policy analysis at times can shape the menu of congressional options through anticipated reactions. Congressional support agencies assist members with the development of policy options, but they may have even more influence by working with the executive branch to flag problems with proposals before they are presented to Congress. One focus group participant told us about how a CBO analysis of problems with a ground combat vehicle that the Pentagon was developing led the Pentagon to significantly scale back the proposal before most members were even aware of it. "Our work sometimes gets into Congress through agencies or the press. We don't necessarily hand an idea to a member and get legislative traction," she said.

Selecting the Criteria

Policy analysis is a value-laden activity. The decision to support or oppose a policy expresses normative judgments about what

TABLE 3

Congress and Evaluative Criteria

Criterion	Key Findings from Literature Review and Survey
Effectiveness	Outside of particularistic programs, MCs rewarded for positions, not effects (Mayhew 1974); instrumental rationality waning (Mayhew 2006)
Economic efficiency	Congress frequently ignores economic efficiency (VanDoren 1989)
Robustness / ease of implementation	MCs not receptive to arguments that something they want to do is not administratively feasible (Derthick 1990)
Fairness	MCs favorite claims appeal to "fair treatment" (Mucciaroni and Quirk 2006)
Budgetary cost	In multivariate analysis, respondents who had been a legislative staff member were more likely to say that cost considerations would affect congressional support for a bill ($p < .01$)
Political acceptability	Congress is responsive to public opinion (survey) and seeks to incorporate popular understandings into policy design (Mayhew 1974)

constitutes good policy. A critical issue is what evaluative criteria Congress brings to bear when considering options to address a problem (see table 3).

For many policy analysts, the most important evaluative criterion is *effectiveness*—whether an option actually helps solve the policy problem (Bardach 2011: 26). In the 1950s and 1960s, members like Wilbur Mills took pride in the craft of legislation (Zelizer 1998). While symbolism has always been a staple of legislative life,

Capitol Hill culture encouraged a seriousness of legislative purpose during this era. In today's Congress, however, it appears that partisanship, ideological rigidity, and the weakening of committees vis-à-vis parties have undermined instrumental activity (Mayhew 2006). Congressional debates are often vehicles for position taking and member advertising rather than opportunities to evaluate the effectiveness of proposed legislation. In their study of congressional deliberation, for example, Mucciaroni and Quirk (2006) found that members of Congress frequently make misleading empirical arguments about the consequences of proposals and only abandon such unsupported claims when there is no longer a political gain from repeating them.[11]

Congress also gives little weight to *economic efficiency*.[12] The usual way that analysts assess efficiency is through cost-benefit (or cost-effectiveness) studies. A majority (54 percent) of survey respondents said that cost-benefit and cost-effectiveness analysis have "only a little" influence on congressional decision making. Twenty-nine percent said these methods have a moderate amount of influence. In multivariate analysis, we found that respondents who reported a high frequency of interactions with members of Congress or congressional staff were *less* likely to believe that cost-benefit studies have a significant impact on Congress ($p < .05$; Appendix 3–1, table 7).[13] This is not to suggest that Congress *prefers* inefficient policies or that there are no conditions under which Congress will vote for Pareto-improving policies (see Arnold 1990). But Congress tends not to value efficiency as an end in itself.

Congress also gives scant attention to what Bardach (2011) calls *robustness*, or the capacity of policies to survive the implementation process. As Martha Derthick (1990: 92) observes, members of Congress are focused on achieving their political goals and are "not receptive to objections that something they want to do is not administratively feasible." Indeed, only 16 percent of survey respondents said that over the past ten years Congress has done a good job of passing bills that can be implemented by the bureaucracy without excessive difficulty.

While Congress tends to downplay effectiveness, efficiency, and administrative feasibility, it often focuses on *fairness*. Based on their review of legislative debates over welfare reform, repeal of the estate tax, and telecommunications deregulation, for example, Mucciaroni and Quirk (2006: 157) argue that "legislators' favorite claims appeal to matters of personal tragedy, struggle or fair treatment, and evoke emotions like envy, resentment and empathy." Members typically devote far more time to discussing the *distributional* consequences of proposals, and whether the outcomes they would produce accord with citizens' views of moral deservingness, than to the proposals' impacts on efficiency (VanDoren 1989). As Schick (1976: 217) notes, "Propelled by pervasive political impulses of 'Who gets what,' Congress seems more concerned about the distributive effects of public policies than about *pro bono publico* benefit-cost ratios. Unlike the analyst who seeks to maximize national welfare, the legislator knows that it is *someone's* welfare that is to be benefited" (emphasis in original). This congressional concern for fairness clearly does not ensure a commitment to reducing income inequality or to equalizing the political influence of the rich and the poor (Bartels 2010; Hacker and Pierson 2011; Gilens 2012; Hochschild 1981). But Congress often concerns itself with assisting groups perceived to be the victims of inequitable treatment. In the debate over whether to subject Internet purchases to sales taxes, for example, Congress was concerned about rectifying "unfairness" to bricks-and-mortar retailers.

Congress also focuses on the budgetary costs of proposals. Thirty percent of the experts in our survey said the cost of the bill would have a lot of influence on the typical member. In multivariate analysis, we found that respondents who had been legislative staff members were more likely to say that cost considerations would affect congressional support for the bill ($p <$ .01; see Appendix 3–1, table 6). As we explain in greater detail below, the CBO has become a key arbiter of the economic consequences of policies, and its analyses of budgetary effects often shape the political context in which proposals are considered (Joyce 2011).

The criterion that Congress weighs most heavily is *political acceptability*. There is no guarantee that this political filter will eliminate only "bad" ideas or ensure that experts' proposals will be adopted. Yet in a democracy political acceptability is a crucial procedural value. Even the most brilliant, expert-certified, Pareto-improving policies cannot be enacted (or sustained) without it. The challenge for experts is that lawmakers are not only responsive to organized groups; they also cater to public opinion and seek to incorporate popular understandings of instrumental rationality into policy design (Mayhew 1974).[14] Counterintuitive proposals that do not reflect common sense tend to be resisted by voters and therefore struggle to gain traction on Capitol Hill (Mayhew 1974). Following the 2008–9 financial crisis, economists had difficulty getting even some Democratic members of Congress to accept the Keynesian argument—which challenged the average citizen's belief about how a family should respond to a period of economic stress—that while the financial crisis was "caused by too much confidence, too much borrowing and lending and too much spending, it can only be resolved with more confidence, more borrowing and lending, and more spending" (Summers 2011).

Yet the resistance of Congress to expert input is not an entirely bad thing in a system of separated powers in which executives and courts tend to more quickly absorb elite thinking. As Mayhew writes:

> The battle between the popular and the high-minded needs to be fought out somewhere. In any society, common sense versus expertise is an opposition that will not go away. In the American system, it is up for grabs how much we are willing to trust scientific, bureaucratic, legal, or moral experts. Congress helps supply an assurance that their ideas need to be sold, not just proclaimed. (2009: 361)

Projecting Outcomes

Policy analysis is *predictive* (Wildavsky 1979). It asks, What will happen if a policy option is enacted? Will a new program deliver on its promises? How much will it cost? And what unintended consequences could it create?

Congress relies heavily on the budget projections of the CBO, which is required by law to produce a formal cost estimate for nearly every bill that is reported by a full committee. By all accounts, CBO budget scores have a massive impact on congressional debate (Joyce 2011). Indeed, a case can be made that CBO budget projections have *too much* influence, sometimes causing members to focus too much on (highly uncertain) short-term budget projections at the expense of an analysis of the broader costs and benefits of a policy option. As one interviewee stated, "CBO cost estimates are very important as it is difficult to get to the floor of the House or Senate without them. It is really the drafts of the cost estimates and mandates that cause committee staff to reconsider approaches. The public seldom sees this happening, but it is very important." There have been many occasions when CBO budget scoring has had a significant impact on the political development and outcome of major reform proposals. One famous example is the CBO's review of President Clinton's health reform plan in 1994 (Joyce 2011). The administration had argued that the plan would save money, but the CBO determined it would increase the deficit. Moreover, while the administration had claimed that the transactions of the health alliances were private and therefore should not be included in the federal budget, the CBO ruled that the transactions were budgetary in nature, making it easier for opponents to argue that the plan would vastly expand federal government activity. Some political analysts believe the CBO's rulings contributed to the demise of the Clinton health plan (Skocpol 1996).

In addition to budget scores, the CBO prepares analytic reports on the effects of legislative proposals at the request of the Congressional leadership or chairmen or ranking members of committees or subcommittees. These reports make no recommendations, but may contain findings that favor one side or another of a political debate. For example, a 1995 CBO report projected that few small businesses and farms would have to be liquidated to pay the estate tax under the rules scheduled to be in effect in 2009 (CBO 1995). A recent history of the CBO, supported by many case examples, concludes that the studies produced by the agency cannot get Congress to do something it does not want to do, though at times it can improve the content of a law that Congress was poised to enact (Joyce 2011).[15] In sum, CBO's budget scores are highly consequential, but its analytic reports have a more circumscribed and contingent impact.

Congress frequently lacks information about potential administrative challenges or weak areas of legislative proposals. Policies that work on paper may not work in practice (Pressman and Wildavsky 1973). Implementation breakdowns not only make it less likely that policy goals will be achieved, but damage the morale and prestige of agencies, although typically not the reputation of legislators themselves.[16] Congress's indifference to implementation concerns appears to have grown over time. An appreciation for the limits of bureaucratic capacity has traditionally resided in committees, but the institutional knowledge base of committees has been weakened by two factors. First, the new Republican majority significantly cut committee staff size in 1995 (Baumgartner and Jones 1995). Second, committee staff turnover increased. "At one time you had staff directors who were there for 10, 15, and 20 years and not only developed a lot of expertise but who would have also worked for both Rs and Ds. Today you have a high rate of turnover," said one analyst we interviewed. According to another expert, "The lack of knowledge about how to implement legislation is becoming a huge problem. This is due to the body becoming more partisan and thus less willing to reach out…. This was a huge problem with [enactment of the] ACA [Affordable Care Act] and it will cause more problems down the line." Because members, unlike presidents, do not have a direct electoral stake in the quality of public administration, there is no procedure to ensure that implementation issues receive attention in legislative debates. To address this gap, Weaver (2000) proposes having the GAO perform "Implementation Analyses" of major legislative proposals, similar to the CBO's budget scoring, but the question remains whether Congress would heed or ignore such reports.

Confronting the Trade-offs

The sixth step of a policy analysis is to confront trade-offs. It sometimes happens that one of the policy options under consideration is expected to produce a better outcome on every relevant economic and political dimension than other alternatives, but that is seldom the case (Bardach 2011). Almost every policy idea is flawed in some way. A typical situation is that Option 1 is projected to make a big dent in solving a problem but would be expensive for the government to carry out; Option 2 has a low budgetary cost but would impose regulatory burdens on small businesses; and Option 3 is popular with voters but won't work. Typically Congress also faces the option to maintain the legislative status quo, which may have been established decades earlier when conditions were quite different.

Does Congress wrestle with such trade-offs in a serious way? Respondents gave Congress low marks on this score: 75 percent disagreed with the statement, "Congress is careful to understand the trade-offs between the outcomes associated with different policy options before deciding on a course of action." The discipline of the budget process forces Congress to accept trade-offs *across* programs, but it seldom compares the relative social welfare benefits of options in an effort to find the best, feasible solution to a given problem. Instead, members of Congress often use the recognition of trade-offs simply to highlight the weaknesses of proposals of the other political party, even if the proposals have net social benefits or were ones that opponents previously endorsed (Lee 2014).

In addition, as Derthick (1990) observes, there is no "budget of administrative capacity" to force Congress to establish sensible implementation priorities. "By definition," she argues, "law is binding; the nature of it is to embody command. Thus, when Congress passes a law containing numerous new provisions, all equally require implementation. The legislature does not stipulate priorities. It does not say, 'If you must choose, do this before that'" (84).

Making Decisions

One of the aims of policy analysis is to inform decisions, but Congress is no ordinary decision-maker. With 535 members, it isn't easy for the institution to act even when a majority agree on a plan. Moreover, legislative rules and procedures erect barriers to change. As Terry M. Moe and Scott A. Wilson (1994: 26–27) have argued, "The transaction costs of moving a bill through the entire legislative process is enormous.... The best prediction is that, for most issues most of the time, there will be no affirmative action on the part of Congress at all. The ideal points may logically support a given outcome, but in reality *nothing will happen*" (emphasis in original). Recent congressional reforms have made lawmaking even more difficult. Historically, one of the ways that coalition leaders have built support for broad-based national legislation is by doling out pork barrel projects to members who vote for the bills (Evans 2004; Ellwood and Patashnik 1993). The recent ban on congressional earmarks, however, has removed some of the vital grease needed to lubricate a creaky legislative process. Yet, despite its reputation as a "gridlocked" institution, Congress has passed sweeping legislation: the American Recovery and Reinvestment Act, the Affordable Care Act, Dodd-Frank, TARP, reform of the federal student loan program, and the Medicare Modernization Act, to give just a few recent examples (Melnick 2013).

From a policy analysis perspective, however, the key issue is not the quantity of decisions Congress makes but their *quality*.[17] Experts we interviewed suggested that the existence of policy analysis informing congressional decision making is not assured by institutionalized practices and norms but rather depends largely on the attitude and involvement of staff who work on the issue. Once bills are drafted by committee staff, there is seldom an opportunity to

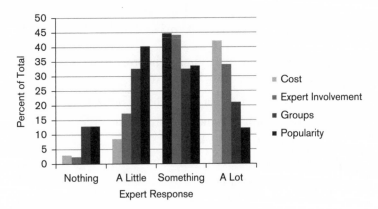

Figure 5. Experts Focus on Cost and Expert Input.

make major revisions. While staff are clearly agents of their respective legislators, they may have considerable discretion regarding what issues they choose to develop. Explained one former senior policy analyst, "The earlier that policy analysts get involved, the larger the impact and the better the policy. This means that generalizations are difficult as the process is lumpy depending on the issue and the staff involved—it can be very good or very bad."

How do members of Congress decide whether to vote for bills? There are clearly important differences between the factors that survey respondents believe members of Congress weigh in making voting decisions and the factors that experts themselves use to evaluate the quality of legislative proposals. The respondents indicated that the most important influences on their own assessments of the quality of a bill are the CBO's estimate of how much the bill will cost (43 percent said this would tell them a lot about the quality of the bill) and whether policy experts played a significant role in the bill's development (34 percent said this would tell them a lot) (figure 5).[18] In contrast, the respondents

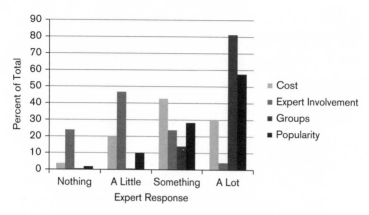

Figure 6. Experts Believe That Members Focus on Groups and Popularity.

perceived that the most important influences on a *typical member of Congress* in deciding whether to support a bill are whether major interest groups are supportive (82 percent of experts said they believed interest group support would have a lot of influence on legislators) and how popular it is with citizens (57 percent of experts said such public support would have a lot of influence on the typical member) (figure 6).

Telling Causal Stories

The final step of a policy analysis is to convince others that the analyst's recommendations are sound. In a democracy, the audience for policy recommendations includes not only elites but also ordinary citizens, who (to press an earlier point) tend to reject ideas that do not reflect common sense. As Bardach (2011) argues, policy analysts must be able to "tell a causal story" linking public problems with proposed solutions (for stories on policy making, see Stone 2001). To be effective, such stories must pass what he calls the "New York Taxi Driver Test" (Bardach 2011: 41): while stalled in New York traffic, the analyst must be able to provide a coherent, easily understood explanation of her policy idea to the typical NYC cabbie before the cabbie loses interest or rejects the idea as yet another scheme of intellectuals to waste taxpayer money. Would-be policy analysts who fail this test prove incapable of "carrying on with the task of public, democratic education" (Bardach 2011: 42).

As Mayhew (2012: 259) notes, "Struggles over causal stories are often at the center of drives to enact legislation." Think of the struggle over the narrative of the Affordable Care Act, or the failed push for Social Security privatization. Members may be challenged to explain proposals to constituents at town hall meetings. On the positive side, the need to tell compelling stories affords members of Congress the opportunity not only to build trust and enhance their political standing, but to play a formative role in the construction of public preferences (Sunstein 1988: 1539–90). Haskins (1991: 618), for example, argues that members built support for welfare reform legislation in the 1990s by telling a plausible causal story that linked citizen dissatisfaction with the increase in welfare spending to the top-down, "federally imposed" structure of the program.

Richard Fenno's (1978) study of members' "homestyles" also highlights the importance of causal explanations. On the basis of participant observation research conducted in the 1970s, Fenno reported that many members believed that their explanations for their votes mattered as much as or more than their roll call votes themselves (see also Kingdon 1997).[19] At times, members of Congress have played a key role not only in explaining their actions to voters in their districts, but in making experts' ideas acceptable to broader publics. For example, in the 1970s, key coalition leaders, such as Ted Kennedy (D-MA), sold microeconomists' proposal for pro-competitive transportation deregulation to the public—over the intense opposition of organized interests—by offering "simple and vivid cues of the merits of the issue"; explaining how vulnerable geographic constituencies (small towns) would be protected from harms; and "making a rhetorical connection between deregulation and larger concerns of the general public," including worries about inflation and Big Government (Derthick and Quirk 1985: 244).

Does the contemporary Congress have a similar capacity to market ideas to the public? The public policy experts in our survey expressed skepticism about members' effectiveness at telling causal stories. Only 19 percent of respondents said that Congress has done a good job or better over the past ten years at explaining policy decisions in commonsense language that ordinary Americans can understand, 35 percent said Congress has done a fair job of explaining policies, and 44 percent said Congress's performance on this dimension has been poor. This poor performance is not due to a lack of assistance from the legislative support agencies. According to a focus group participant, agencies like CRS offer a lot of help to members who know there is a problem but do not know how to fix it or how to explain a technical policy solution to voters. "Case in point is the rising salinity of the ocean," this participant said. "A liberal member knows this is a problem but has no idea what options are to solve it. Policy analysis helps him to claim credit (I have a solution), take a position (we need to lower the temperature of the ocean), and explain causal action (if we don't do this, we won't be able to continue commercial fishing off the coast of our state)." If the public mistrusts Congress, however, the persuasive influence of members will be constrained.

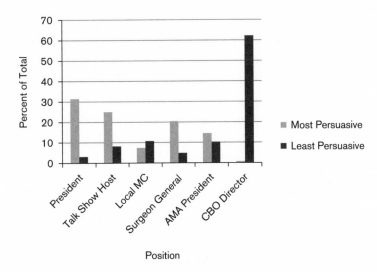

Figure 7. Expert Assessments of Relative Persuasiveness.

As a gauge of how effective experts believe members are at telling convincing stories, we asked them to consider the case of convincing the average citizen that a recently enacted public health law was necessary and in the public interest. As figure 7 shows, respondents overwhelmingly believed that the local of member of Congress would be less persuasive to the average citizen not only than the U.S. president and the president of the American Medical Association but also than a radio talk show host. The CBO director was perceived to have no ability to persuade the public about the need for the program.

What Does Congress Not Do Poorly?

As we have seen, our survey respondents gave Congress low marks as a problem-solving institution. This is unsurprising. Policy analysts (especially those who work in universities and think tanks) are tough critics, and Congress is a disparaged institution. In the face of these negative reviews, does the survey say *anything* positive at all about Congress's contribution to problem solving?

Another way to interrogate our results is to ask not what experts believe Congress does well but what they believe Congress at least does not do poorly. Here the results are illuminating. As table 4 shows, experts overwhelmingly agreed that Congress's performance over the past decade has *not* been poor at avoiding negative consequences for business, satisfying interest groups, reflecting public opinion, and bringing attention to new issues. These are not insignificant contributions to problem solving in a political system in which different institutions and actors bring different strengths. A concern for public opinion, for example, is essential if people are to accept the outcomes of policy decisions.[20] More striking is that a clear majority of experts did not give Congress poor marks on key tasks, including achieving policy goals at acceptable cost, reflecting the ideas of policy experts, and passing bills the bureaucracy can handle without difficulty. (For the most part, the experts rated Congress's performance as "only fair" in these areas.) The performance dimensions on which an overwhelming majority of experts found Congress's record poor are distributing benefits equitably across income groups, taking into account the interests of future generations, and making evidence-based decisions. Two-thirds of respondents believed that Congress is dismal at those tasks.

CONCLUSION

Congress's performance as a policy analyst is problematic to say the least, but it is important to appraise the institution against a

TABLE 4

Experts Reporting Poor Congressional Performance on ...	Percent of Total
Pleasing Interest Groups	1
Avoiding Negative Consequences for Business	9
Reflecting Public Opinion	15
Bringing Attention to New Issues	21
Distributing Benefits Equitably Across Districts	33
Achieving Policy Objectives at Acceptable Cost	34
Reflecting Ideas of Policy Experts	35
Passing Bills that the Bureaucracy Can Handle	36
Promoting Economic Efficiency	43
Explaining Decisions in Ordinary Language	45
Developing New Policy Options	48
Targeting Resources Effectively	50
Defining Problems Logically	56
Distributing Benefits Equitably Across Income Groups	62
Taking Into Account the Interests of Future Generations	65
Making Evidence-Based Decisions	66

reasonable set of expectations. Policy analysis involves (and should involve) intelligence *and* social interaction (Wildavsky 1979). Once Congress's performance is broken down into discrete tasks—something that previous research on the subject has not done—it becomes clear that Congress is neither estranged from policy analysis nor consumed by it. Great efforts have been made over the past half century to boost Congress's analytic capacity through the establishment of support agencies like the CBO. The contemporary Congress clearly possesses the information and access to expertise required to absorb social science findings and craft thoughtful solutions. What is arguably needed to improve Congress's performance as a problem-solving institution are not additional analytic boosters but rather changes in legislative norms and practices (such as reducing the number of complex omnibus bills covering diverse subjects) to promote a "culture of problem solving on Capitol Hill" (Mayhew 2006: 230).

Overall, survey respondents gave Congress low marks on tasks involving the use of knowledge, such as making policy decisions on the basis of evidence. At the same time, their responses point to some areas of *relative* institutional strength, such as Congress's ability to craft policies that reflect public opinion. The most troubling results of the survey, in our view, touch not on Congress's lack of interest in cost-benefit analysis, which is old news, but rather on the perception among many experts that the institution today is not contributing as much as it might to the representational and legitimating sides of problem solving. This can be seen, for example, in the belief among many respondents that Congress has done a poor job of explaining issues to mass publics in plain language or developing solutions that the citizenry can understand and embrace. The quality of governance depends on the efficiency of policy choices, but it also depends on the accountability relationship between legislators and citizens.

Several issues require more attention. The first is the influence of polarization and party competition on congressional performance. The literature on partisan polarization has focused on its impact on legislative productivity as measured by the quantity of laws passed, but we need more fine-grained evidence on how polarization and party competition affects the quality of deliberation, the definition of problems, and the way that Congress incorporates expertise and uses information (Quirk 2011).

The standard process by which expertise influences policy making in the United States is through elite-led social learning. Policy experts first reach a scientific consensus on a technical issue, which then diffuses down to policy makers and the general public (Zaller 1992). This elite-led social learning process is mediated, however, by the structure of electoral competition between the two parties. The current political era is characterized by a polarization of policy elites, a sorting of constituencies, and the longest period of parity in party competition since the Civil War (Lee 2014). In this combative environment, each party has a strong electoral incentive to attack the proposals of the other side, even in the absence of an underlying substantive disagreement about public policy (Lee 2014). Gerber and Patashnik (2011) have argued that even bipartisan, technocratic reform ideas like evidence-based medicine may become the objects of political contestation. We need to learn more about the conditions under which such politicization of expertise emerges, and what if any countervailing forces might suppress it.

While the focus of this chapter is on how Congress's capacities vary across eight dimensions of policy analysis, a key issue for inquiry is whether and how Congress's use of policy analysis varies across policy sectors (Katznelson and Lapinski 2008). Is it the case, for example, that Congress's use of policy analysis is better in the defense arena than in domestic sectors (Schick 1976)? How is the willingness of Congress to confront trade-offs shaped by the density of think tanks and experts in particular arenas? Do senior staff and members of congressional support agencies systematically skew the advice they give to members of Congress to comport with Congress's strongly instrumental approach when issues directly implicate members' reelection concerns? How severe is this skewing? How much rationality seeps through, and does this vary in any systematic way across policy domains?

A third issue concerns the variation in congressional performance over time. There is nothing remotely new about elite complaints about Congress's failure to follow expertise.[21] Yet Congress's performance as a problem-solving institution seems to have atrophied in recent decades (Mayhew 2006). At earlier moments in American history, Congress appeared to have the capacity to address the issues on its agenda, including big social conflicts like civil rights, yet today the congressional agenda is dominated by technical issues, where Congress does not seem as well suited to act. At the same time, expectations of political fairness and economic performance have become more exacting. How have congressional tools to reconcile the pressures of democratic politics with the dictates of policy analysis been affected by the new kinds of political demands and issue contexts we are confronting today? Does Congress end up focusing on more technical issues because its analytic capacity has grown—or because secular trends like polarization, the closeness of electoral competition between the two parties, and globalization have weakened the institution's ability to deal with larger challenges? Our sense is that Congress's agenda is driven more by presidential leadership, policy feedback from past decisions, and electoral pressures than by the growth of its analytic machinery, but the necessary research has not been conducted.

A final issue concerns the separation of powers.[22] The idealized view of the institutional relationship in modern American government suggests that Congress "owns" the representation function while the executive branch "owns" most technocratic governing capacity. From this perspective, many scholars believe that stark differences remain between Congress and the executive in both orientation and performance. In his recent book on why domestic policies go awry, for example, Peter Schuck (2014: 169) argues that congressional defects and dysfunction are the main institutional source of government failure, while administrative agencies remain the "best loci within the government of fine-grained policy analysis." Yet other scholars argue that the thrust of institutional development over the past half century—including the expanded representational role of the presidency, agencies, and courts—has been to erode the separation of powers and functional differences among the branches. To evaluate the consequences of Congress's work as a policy analyst, we therefore need to understand not only how Congress's roles and capacities have changed but also how other institutions have responded to Congress's evolution. Have the other branches found ways to enhance (or offset) the strengths (and limitations) of Congress's contributions to problem solving? Or are the virtues (and defects) of our political institutions today mutually reinforcing? Answering these questions will reveal not only how public policy is made in American government, but to what ends.

TABLE 5

Determinants of the Belief That Congress Fails to Reflect Public Opinion

Explanatory Variable	Model 1	Model 2	Model 3
Legislative Staffer	−0.35** (0.16)	−0.37** (0.17)	−0.36** (0.17)
Party Identification	0.21*** (0.06)	—	0.18*** (0.06)
Ideology	0.06 (0.06)	−0.01 (0.05)	—
Female	−0.002 (0.14)	0.04 (.14)	−0.02 (.14)
Constant	2.32*** (0.61)	3.73*** (0.17)	2.69*** (0.54)
R²	0.10	0.03	0.10
N	155	155	155

NOTE:

All tests run using OLS regression. Robust standard errors in parenthesis.

* $p < .10$, ** $p < .05$, *** $p < .01$ (two-tailed tests)

Models were also run using ordered logistic regression, and the results were nearly identical.

TABLE 6

Determinants of the Belief That the Cost of a Bill Influences Votes

Explanatory Variable	Model 1	Model 2	Model 3
Legislative Staffer	0.49*** (0.14)	0.49*** (0.14)	0.51*** (0.14)
Party Identification	−0.03 (0.05)	—	−0.04 (0.05)
Ideology	0.02 (0.05)	0.03 (0.05)	—
Female	0.15 (0.13)	0.15 (.13)	0.18 (.14)
Constant	3.04*** (0.36)	2.85*** (0.15)	3.17*** (0.31)
R^2	0.06	0.06	0.06
N	157	157	157

NOTE:

All tests run using OLS regression. Robust standard errors in parenthesis.

* $p < .10$, ** $p < .05$, *** $p < .01$ (two-tailed tests)

Models were also run using ordered logistic regression and the results were nearly identical.

TABLE 7

Determinants of the Belief That Cost-Benefit Studies Influence Congress

Explanatory Variable	Model 1	Model 2	Model 3
Frequent Interactions with Congress	−0.42** (0.17)	−0.45*** (0.17)	−0.41** (0.17)
Party Identification	−0.06 (0.08)	−0.05 (0.07)	—
Ideology	−0.01 (0.06)	—	0.01 (0.06)
Female	0.22 (0.19)	0.24 (0.18)	0.21 (0.18)
Constant	3.10*** (0.56)	3.04*** (0.40)	2.71*** (0.24)
R^2	0.04	0.05	0.04
N	155	155	155

NOTE:

All tests run using OLS regression. Robust standard errors in parenthesis.

* $p < .10$, ** $p < .05$, *** $p < .01$ (two-tailed tests)

Models were also run using ordered logistic regression and the results were nearly identical.

TABLE 8

Determinants of the Belief That Committee Chairs Would Learn of Academic Study

Explanatory Variable	Model 1	Model 2	Model 3
Legislative Staffer	0.37 (0.24)	0.37 (0.23)	0.38* (0.21)
Party Identification	0.08 (0.07)	—	0.06 (0.06)
Ideology	0.03 (0.07)	0.01 (0.06)	—
Female	−0.12 (0.16)	−0.1 (.16)	−0.11 (.16)
Constant	1.82*** (0.57)	2.38*** (0.21)	2.02*** (0.38)
R^2	0.03	0.02	0.03
N	157	157	157

NOTE:

All tests run using OLS regression. Robust standard errors in parenthesis.

* $p < .10$, ** $p < .05$, *** $p < .01$ (two-tailed tests)

Models were also run using ordered logistic regression, and the results were nearly identical.

SURVEY TEXT

Q2 Informed Consent You are being asked to complete an online research survey that will take approximately 12 minutes. Participation is voluntary and you do not have to answer any questions you don't want to answer. You are free to stop the survey at any time without penalty. If you have any questions about your rights as a research participant or concerns about the conduct of this study, you may contact the University of Virginia Institutional Review Board for Social & Behavioral Sciences at 434–924–5999.

I agree to participate (1)

I do not agree to participate (2)

Q 3 Please think about the overall performance of Congress over the last decade. To what extent do you agree or disagree with each statement below?

Strongly Disagree (1)   Disagree (2)

Neither Disagree nor Agree (3)   Agree (4)

Strongly Agree (5)   Don't Know (6)

Congress does not rely on expert research as much as it should (1)

Congress is careful to understand the tradeoffs between the outcomes associated with different policy options before deciding on a course of action (2)

Congress is more concerned with looking good in the eyes of voters than with actually solving problems (3)

Congress is effective at crafting solutions to national problems that the public can understand and live with. (4)

Q 4 Policy experts often make judgments about the quality of bills passed by the Congress. Please tell me how much you think each of the following kinds of information would tell you about whether a specific bill passed by Congress is a good or bad bill. Would this tell you nothing, a little, something, or a lot about the quality of the bill?

Nothing (1)   A Little (2)
Something (3)   A Lot (4)
Unsure (5)

Whether the bill has bipartisan support (1)

Whether the president supports the bill (2)

Whether public policy experts played a significant role in the bill's development (3)

How popular the bill is with citizens (4)

The Congressional Budget Office's estimate of how much the bill will cost to implement (5)

Whether other nations have adopted similar measures (6)

Whether the New York Times editorial board endorsed the bill (7)

Whether major interest groups support the bill (8)

Whether the bill was recommended by a blue ribbon commission of distinguished leaders (9)

Q5 Please tell me how much you think each of the following kinds of informa-tion would influence a typical member of Congress in deciding whether to vote for a specific bill. Do you think each would influence the typical legislator not very much, a little, some, or a lot?

Whether the bill has bipartisan support (1)

Whether the president supports the bill (2)

Whether public policy experts played a significant role in the bill's development (3)

How popular the bill is with citizens (4)

The Congressional Budget Office's estimate of how much the bill will cost to implement (5)

Whether other nations have adopted similar measures (6)

Whether the New York Times editorial board endorsed the bill (7)

Whether major interest groups support the bill (8)

Whether the bill was recommended by a blue ribbon commis-sion of distinguished leaders (9)

Q6 Suppose that Congress has passed a law costing $1 billion to mitigate a pub-lic health problem that most citizens know nothing about. After the law's enact-ment, various actors make public statements about the law. Which of the following actors do you think would be most effective at persuading the average citizen that the law's enactment was necessary and in the national interest?

Talk radio host (1)

The U.S. President (2)

The member of Congress who represents the citizen's district (3)

The Surgeon General (4)

The president of the American Medical Association (5)

The director of the Congressional Budget Office (6)

Q7 Which of the following actors do you think would be least effective at persuading the average citizen that the law's enactment was necessary and in the national interest

Talk radio host (1)

The U.S. President (2)

The member of Congress who represents the citizen's district (3)

The Surgeon General (4)

The president of the American Medical Association (5)

The director of the Congressional Budget Office (6)

Q8 Suppose a prestigious academic journal publishes a research study that shows that a federal transportation program is highly cost-ineffective, meaning that it would be possible to achieve the same transportation benefits at much lower cost, or to spend the same amount of money while generating much larger transportation benefits.

Not at all confident (1)   A little confident (2)

Somewhat confident (3)   Very confident (4)

Unsure (5)

How confident are you that the chairs of the congressional committees with jurisdiction over the transportation program would become aware of this research study? (1)

How confident are you that Congress would make a serious attempt to replace the existing transportation program with a more cost-effective approach? (2)

Q9 In the past 10 years, how good a job do you think that Congress has done on . . .

Excellent (1)   Very Good (2)

Good (3)   Only fair (4)

Poor (5)   Not sure (6)

Bringing political attention to new issues (1)

Defining public policy problems in ways that are logical and
analytically manageable (2)

Making policy decisions on the basis of objective evidence (3)

Developing new policy options for addressing national
problems (4)

Explaining policy decisions in ordinary, commonsense language
that the public can understand (5)

*Q10 In the past 10 years how good a job do you think that Congress has done at
passing bills that*

Excellent (1)   Very good (2)

Good (3)   Only fair (4)

Poor (5)   Unsure (6)

Promote economic efficiency (1)

Distribute the benefits of government programs equitably across
geographic jurisdictions (2)

Distribute the benefits of government programs equitably across
income groups (3)

Achieve their policy objectives at acceptable cost (4)

Reflect the ideas of policy experts (5)

Reflect public opinion (6)

Are acceptable to interest groups (7)

Are able to be implemented by the bureaucracy without
excessive difficulty (8)

Avoid negative consequences for businesses (9)

Target public resources efficiently and minimize waste and
abuse (10)

Take into the account the interests of future generations (11)

Q11 Which of the following statements do you agree with more? Statement 1: Congressional leaders often do not know the best way to address national problems, and look to policy experts for guidance on the most effective course of action Statement 2: Congressional leaders usually know how they wish to address national problems, and they use the recommendations of policy experts to add legitimacy to positions they would have taken anyway

Agree with Statement 1 more (1)

Agree with Statement 2 more (2)

Agree equally with both statements (3)

Don't agree with either statement (4)

Don't know, unsure (5)

Q12 Sometimes Congress fails to take steps to address an important domestic problem. Here is a list of some things that could cause Congress to fail as a problem-solving institution. For each one, please indicate how important you believe each one has been over the last decade.

Extremely Important (1)   Very Important (2)

Somewhat Important (3)   Not too important (4)

Unsure (5)

Partisan polarization (1)

Lawmakers focused on their own reelection (2)

Lack of good information about how to solve problems (3)

Interest group pressure (4)

Failure of voters to hold Congress accountable for its collective
    performance (5)

Filibuster and other procedural hurdles (6)

Problems are very complicated (7)

Q13 How often do members of Congress seek to learn from the best practices and policy successes of state governments when they craft legislation?

Never (1)

Almost Never (2)

Sometimes (3)

Fairly Often (4)

Very Often (5)

Don't Know (6)

Q14 How often do members of Congress seek to learn from the best practices and policy successes of other nations when they craft legislation?

Never (1)

Almost Never (2)

Sometimes (3)

Fairly Often (4)

Very Often (5)

Don't Know (6)

Q15 How much impact do cost-benefit or cost-effectiveness studies have on congressional decision-making

None at all (1)

A little (2)

A moderate amount (3)

A lot (4)

A great deal (5)

Don't know (6)

Q16 Do you think that important domestic policy decisions should be made by the Congress or by the President?

Only the Congress (1)

Mostly the Congress, with some input the President (2)

The Congress and the President equally (3)

Mostly the President, with some input from Congress (4)

Only the President (5)

Don't know (6)

Q17 Do you think that important foreign policy decisions should be made by the Congress or by the President?

Only the Congress (1)

Mostly the Congress, with some input the President (2)

The Congress and the President equally (3)

Mostly the President, with some input from Congress (4)

Only the President (5)

Don't know (6)

Q18 Where do you work? (CHECK ALL THAT APPLY)

Federal executive branch (1)

Federal legislative branch (2)

Federal court system (3)

State or local government (4)

Think tank or research organization (5)

Foundation (6)

University or college (7)

Advocacy organization (8)

Government contractor (9)

Nonprofit service provider (10)

Other (11) _____

Q19 Have you ever served in a legislature or on a legislative staff?

Yes (1)

No (2)

Q20 In the past five years, how often have you had occasion to interact directly with members of Congress or with congressional staff?

Once a month or more (1)

Several times a year (2)

About once a year (3)

On occasion, but less than once a year (4)

Never (5)

Not sure (6)

Q21 We hear a lot of talk these days about liberals and conservatives. Here is a 7-point scale on which the political views that people might hold are arranged from extremely liberal to extremely conservative. Where would you place yourself on this scale, or haven't you thought much about this?

Extremely Liberal (1)

Liberal (2)

Slightly Liberal (3)

Moderate, Middle of the Road (4)

Slightly Conservative (5)

Conservative (6)

Extremely Conservative (7)

Haven't thought about it much (8)

Does not apply/Don't wish to answer (9)

Q22 Generally speaking, do you usually think of yourself as a Republican, a Democrat, or an Independent, or what?

Strong Republican (1)

Republican (2)

Independent, Lean Republican (3)

Independent (4)

Independent, Lean Democratic (5)

Democrat (6)

Strong Democrat (7)

Other (8) _____

Don't wish to answer (9)

Q23 What is your gender?

Female (1)

Male (2)

Q24 What is your highest education level?

High School graduate or less (1)

College Graduate (2)

Master's or Professional Degree (3)

Doctorate (4)

If High School graduate or less Is Selected, Then Skip To End of Block If College Graduate Is Selected, Then Skip To End of Block

Q25 What field was your highest degree earned in? (CHECK ALL THAT APPLY)

Economics (1)

Political Science (2)

Public Administration (3)

Public Policy (4)

Sociology (5)

Law (6)

Business (7)

Other (8) _____

NOTES

1. We thus distinguish between client-based policy analysis and policy research. On the similarities and differences between these activities, see Weimer and Vining 1999.

2. On the technical side of policy analysis, see Vining and Weimer 2010. For an insightful review of the evolution of the profession of policy analysis, see Radin (2000).

3. APPAM and UVA employees were excluded from the survey invitation list.

4. Respondents had a different view when it comes to important foreign policy decisions. A majority (54 percent) said such decisions should be made mostly by the president, with some input from Congress.

5. While the N is very small, the 10 self-identified Republicans / lean Republican respondents who answered this question had similar assessments to the overall sample. Six of 10 rated Congress's problem defining performance as poor and 4 as fair.

6. This is not to say Congress never uses expertise to reconceptualize problems. As a staff member of the House Subcommittee on Elections in the late 1980s, Patashnik corresponded with the political scientist Raymond Wolfinger about his empirical research on the causes of low voter turnout. Contrary to the widely held belief that low voter turnout reflected political alienation and mistrust in government, Wolfinger's research suggested that a more prosaic reason why some citizens did not vote was because they were residentially mobile and failed to update their voter registration information following a change of address. Wolfinger's research helped reframe the problem of low voter turnout among congressional staffers working on the issue, leading to the enactment of the National Voter Registration Act of 1993 (the "motor-voter" bill). See Wolfinger 1991.

7. This is broadly consistent with Kingdon's (1997) finding that solutions may chase problems as the policy agenda is formed rather than the other way around.

8. At times, experts who work for congressional support agencies face hard questions about how to balance responsibility to their clients and analytic integrity (see Fisher 2011). Having Congress as one's boss

is certainly not easy, but policy analysts (no matter who their client is) struggle with such professional dilemmas all the time. "Analysts must expect ... that their clients will be players in the game of politics—players who not only have their own personal conceptions of the good society but who almost always must acknowledge the often narrow interests of their constituencies if they hope to remain the in the game" (Weimer and Vining 1999: 44).

9. "Pareto-improving" is an economic term meaning that at least some groups are made better off and that no groups are made worse off.

10. Of course, even if the committee chair does not learn of the study, it is possible her staff would. During the 99th Congress (1985–87), Whiteman surveyed congressional staff about their awareness of specific policy analysis reports. He found considerable variance, but in most issue areas over 80 percent of the staff members were aware of the relevant studies, and only one project showed less than 50 percent awareness. Interestingly, Whiteman found an inverse relationship between the perceived constituency interest in an issue and familiarity with policy analysis: on issues salient to the constituency, congressional offices tend to rely more heavily on constituent views and do not seek out other sources of information (Whiteman 1985: 162–63).

11. Of course, there are exceptions to the rule that Congress is less interested in policy effectiveness. Several analysts we interviewed independently pointed to the design of the 2009 economic stimulus legislation as a counterexample. Senators from natural resource states like North Dakota that were suffering less from the Great Recession were willing to embrace a Medicaid formula that targeted funds at hardest hit states in an effort to blunt the pro-cyclical budget cuts of the states and boost the national recovery, even though this meant their states would be losers under the formula. But it is difficult to maintain a congressional focus on effectiveness outside national crises.

12. The literature has identified many factors that may cause government to pay little attention to economic efficiency, including: reelection incentives, geographically based constituencies, the influence of interest groups, electoral cycles, and the tendency of voters to treat losses and gains asymmetrically (Weimer and Vining 2006).

13. When members of Congress *do* actively push for greater use of cost-benefit analysis, they often do so in a selective way, to erect procedural barriers against policies disfavored on ideological or partisan grounds. For example, House Republicans who wanted to neuter financial reform proposed that the Security and Exchange Commission conduct cost-benefit studies of its rule makings (Haberkorn 2013). It should be emphasized that cost-benefit analyses conducted by the executive branch may leave a significant imprint on congressional decision making. See Hird 1991.

14. In multivariate analysis, we found that survey respondents who reported having served on a legislative staff or in a legislature were more likely ($p <$ .05) to say that Congress does a good job of reflecting public opinion than those who have not served on a legislative staff or in a legislature. (See table 5.)

15. It is sometimes claimed that a role of the support agencies is to stop bad ideas, but it is unclear how frequently this happens. Certainly there are examples of the support agencies' work improving legislation. For example, the Carter energy proposal changed as a result of a CBO analysis (Joyce 2011).

16. Fiorina (1977) famously suggested that members of Congress *want* the bureaucracy to perform poorly, so they can come to the rescue of aggrieved citizens.

17. In addition to welfare economics and public administration lenses for evaluating the quality of statutes (Frankel and Orszag 2002; Light 2002), political scientists have recently begun to focus on policy sustainability (see Patashnik 2008; Patashnik and Zelizer 2013; Maltzman and Shipan 2008; Jenkins and Patashnik 2012; Berry, Burden, and Howell 2010).

18. Just 11 percent of survey respondents said that a *New York Times* editorial board endorsement would tell them a lot about the quality of a bill. To the extent such editorials give respondents new information, this finding implies that while professional policy analysts skew to the left, they are not reflexive liberals.

19. In today's more polarized environment, however, it may be more challenging for members to come up with explanations that will satisfy both primary and general election voters, unless they are able to successfully tailor their messages and communications to suit

different audiences (on tailoring of legislators' explanations, see Mayhew 1974).

20. As Wildavsky (1979: 406) wrote, "Nor do I believe policy analysis is a waste of time, because no one cares what is true and beautiful but only what is popular and preferable. Popularity in a democracy is no mean recommendation; a policy that is marginally preferable has much to commend it compared to one that is perfectly impossible."

21. In the nineteenth century, Mark Twain famously quipped, "Suppose you were an idiot, and suppose you were a member of Congress; but I repeat myself" (Paine 1912: 724).

22. We thank Stephen Skowronek for stimulating us to think about this issue.

REFERENCES

Adler, E. Scott, and John D. Wilkerson. 2012. *Congress and the Politics of Policymaking.* New York: Cambridge University Press.

Arnold, R. Douglas. 1990. *The Logic of Congressional Action.* New Haven, CT: Yale University Press.

Bardach, Eugene. 2011. *A Practical Guide for Policy Analysis: The Eightfold Path to More Effective Problem Solving.* 4th ed. Washington, DC: CQ Press.

Bartels, Larry. 2010. *Unequal Democracy: The Political Economy of the New Gilded Age.* Princeton, NJ: Princeton University Press.

Baumgartner, Frank R., and Bryan D. Jones. 2015. *The Politics of Information: Problem Definition and the Course of Public Policy in America.* Chicago: University of Chicago Press.

Berry, Christopher R., Barry C. Burden, and William G. Howell. 2010. "After Enactment: The Lives and Deaths of Federal Programs." *American Journal of Political Science* 54 (1): 1–17.

Bimber, Bruce. 1991. "Information as a Factor in Congressional Politics." *Legislative Studies Quarterly* 16 (November): 585–605.

———. 1996. *The Politics of Expertise in Congress: The Rise and Fall of the Office of Technology Assessment.* Albany: State University of New York Press.

Becker, Gary. 1983. "A Theory of Competition among Pressure Groups for Political Influence." *Quarterly Journal of Economics* 98: 371–400.

Cohen, Jeffrey E. 2012. *The President's Legislative Policy Agenda, 1789–2002*. New York: Cambridge University Press.

Congressional Budget Office. 1995. "Who Pays and When? An Assessment of Generational Accounting." www.cbo.gov/sites/default/files/cbofiles/attachments/Genacct.pdf.

Derthick, Martha. 1990. *Agency under Stress*. Washington, DC: Brookings Institution.

Derthick, Martha, and Paul J. Quirk. 1985. *The Politics of Deregulation*. Washington, DC: Brookings Institution.

Drutman, Lee, and Steven M. Teles. 2015. "A New Agenda for Political Reform." *Washington Monthly*. (Online). http://washingtonmonthly.com/magazine/maraprmay-2015/a-new-agenda-for-political-reform/.

Easterling, Kevin. 2004. *The Political Economy of Expertise: Information and Efficiency in American National Politics*. Ann Arbor: University of Michigan Press.

Ellwood, John W., and Eric M. Patashnik. 1993. "In Praise of Pork." *National Affairs* 110: 19–33.

Fisher, Louis. 2011. *Defending Congress and the Constitution*. Lawrence: University Press of Kansas.

Fenno, Richard F. 1978. *Home Style: House Members in Their Districts*. New York: Longman.

Fiorina, Morris P. 1977. "The Case of Vanishing Marginals: The Bureaucracy Did It." *American Political Science Review* 71 (March): 177–81.

Frankel, Jeffrey A., and Peter R. Orszag. 2002. *American Economic Policy in the 1990s*. Cambridge, MA: MIT Press.

Gerber, Alan S., and Eric M. Patashnik, eds. 2006a. *Promoting the General Welfare: New Perspectives on Government Performance*. Washington, DC: Brookings Institution.

———. 2006b. "Sham Surgery: The Problem of Inadequate Medical Evidence." In Alan S. Gerber and Eric M. Patashnik, eds., *Promoting the General Welfare: New Perspectives on Government Performance*, 43–73. Washington, DC: Brookings Institution.

————. 2011. "The Politicization of Evidence-Based Medicine: The Limits of Pragmatic Problem Solving in an Era of Polarization." *California Journal of Politics and Policy* 3 (4): 1–14.

Gilens, Martin. 2012. *Affluence and Influence: Economic Inequality and Political Power in America.* Princeton, NJ: Princeton University Press.

Haberkorn, Jennifer. 2013. "Eric Cantor Pledges Another Obamacare Repeal Vote." *Politico,* May 3. Available at www.politico.com/story /2013/05/obamacare-repeal-vote-eric-cantor-90900.html.

Hacker, Jacob S., and Paul Pierson. 2011. *Winner-Take-All Politics: How Washington Made the Rich Richer—and Turned Its Back on the Middle Class.* New York: Simon and Schuster.

Hall, Richard L., and Alan V. Deardorff. 2006. "Lobbying as Legislative Subsidy." *American Political Science Review* 100, no. 1 (February): 69–84.

Haskins, Ron. 1991. "Congress Writes a Law: Research and Welfare Reform." *Journal of Policy Analysis and Management* 10: 616–32.

Heclo, H. Hugh. 1972. "Policy Analysis." *British Journal of Political Science* 2 (January): 83–108.

Hird, John A. 1991. "The Political Economy of Pork: Project Selection at the United States Army Corps of Engineers." *American Political Science Review* 85 (Spring): 429–56.

————. 2005. *Power, Knowledge, and Politics: Policy Analysis in the States.* Washington, DC: Georgetown University Press.

Hochschild, Jennifer. 1981. *What's Fair? American Beliefs about Distributive Justice.* Cambridge, MA: Harvard University Press.

Jenkins, Jeffery A., and Eric M. Patashnik, eds. 2012. *Living Legislation: Durability, Change, and the Politics of American Lawmaking.* Chicago: University of Chicago Press.

Jones, Charles O. 1976. "Why Congress Can't Do Policy Analysis (or words to that effect)." *Policy Analysis* 2: 251–64.

Joyce, Philip G. 2011. *The Congressional Budget Office: Honest Numbers, Power, and Policymaking.* Washington, DC: Georgetown University Press.

Katznelson, Ira, and John S. Lapinski. 2006. "At the Crossroads: Congress and American Political Development." *Perspectives on Politics* 4: 243–60.

Kingdon, John W. 1997. *Agendas, Alternatives, and Public Policies.* 2nd ed. New York: Addison-Wesley Educational Publishers.

Krehbiel, Keith. 1991. *Information and Legislative Organization.* Ann Arbor: University of Michigan Press.

Lee, Frances E. 2005. "Interests, Constituencies, and Policy Making." In Paul J. Quirk and Sarah A. Binder, eds., *The Legislative Branch,* 281–313. New York: Oxford University Press.

———. 2009. *Beyond Ideology: Politics, Principles, and Partisanship in the U.S. Senate.* Chicago: University of Chicago Press.

———. 2014. "American Politics Is More Competitive than Ever: That's Making Partisanship Worse," *Washington Post,* January 9. www.washingtonpost.com/blogs/monkey-cage/wp/2014/01/09/american-politics-is-more-competitive-than-ever-thats-making-partisanship-worse/.

Light, Paul C. 2002. *Government's Greatest Achievements: From Civil Rights to Homeland Security.* Washington, DC: Brookings Institution Press.

Lindblom, Charles E. 1959. "The Science of 'Muddling Through.'" *Public Administration Review* 19 (Spring): 79–88.

Maltzman, Forrest, and Charles R. Shipan. 2008. "Continuity, Change, and the Evolution of the Law." *American Journal of Political Science* 52 (April): 252–67.

Mann, Thomas E., and Norman J. Ornstein. 2012. *It's Even Worse than It Looks: How the American Constitutional System Collided with the New Politics of Extremism.* New York: Basic Books.

Mayhew, David R. 1974. *Congress: The Electoral Connection.* New Haven, CT: Yale University Press.

———. 2006. "Congress as Problem Solver." In Alan Gerber and Eric M. Patashnik, eds., *Promoting the General Welfare: New Perspectives on Government Performance,* 219–37. Washington, DC: Brookings Institution Press.

———. 2009. "Is Congress 'the Broken Branch'?" *Boston University Law Review* 89: 357–69.

———. 2012. "Lawmaking as a Cognitive Enterprise." In Jeffery A. Jenkins and Eric M. Patashnik, eds., *Living Legislation: Durability, Change, and the Politics of American Lawmaking,* 255–65. Chicago: University of Chicago Press.

Melnick, R. Shep. 2013. "The Gridlock Illusion." *Wilson Quarterly* (Winter). (Online). http://wilsonquarterly.com/quarterly/winter-2013-is-democracy-worth-it/the-gridlock-illusion/.

Meltsner, Arnold. 1976. *Policy Analysts in the Bureaucracy.* Berkeley: University of California Press.

Moe, Terry M. 1985. "The Politicized Presidency." In John E. Chubb and Paul E. Peterson, eds., *The New Direction in American Politics,* 235–72. Washington, DC: Brookings Institution Press.

Moe, Terry M., and Scott A. Wilson. 1994. "Presidents and the Politics of Structure." *Law and Contemporary Problems* 57: 1–44.

Mucciaroni, Gary, and Paul J. Quirk. 2006. *Deliberative Choices: Debating Public Policy in Congress.* Chicago: University of Chicago Press.

Nivola, Pietro S., and David W. Brady. 2008. *Red and Blue Nation? Consequences and Correction of America's Polarized Politics.* Washington, DC: Brookings Institution Press.

Paine, Albert Bigelow. 1912. *Mark Twain: A Biography.* New York: Dodo Press.

Patashnik, Eric M. 2008. *Reforms at Risk: What Happens after Major Policy Changes Are Enacted.* Princeton, NJ: Princeton University Press.

Patashnik, Eric M., and Julian E. Zelizer. 2013. "The Struggle to Remake Politics: Liberal Reform and the Limits of Policy Feedback in the Contemporary American State." *Perspectives on Politics* (December): 1071–87.

Peterson, Mark A. 1995. "How Health Policy Information Is Used in Congress." In Thomas E. Mann and Norman J. Ornstein, eds., *Intensive Care: How Congress Shapes Health Policy.* Washington, DC: AEI and Brookings Institution.

Pierson, Paul. 1993. "When Effect Becomes Cause: Policy Feedback and Political Change." *World Politics* 45 (4): 595–628.

Polsby, Nelson W. 1969. "Policy Analysis and Congress." *Public Policy* 18 (Fall): 61–74.

Pressman, Jeffrey L., and Aaron Wildavsky. 1973. *Implementation: How Great Expectations in Washington are Dashed in Oakland; Or, Why It's Amazing That Federal Programs Work at All, This Being a Saga of the Economic Development Administration as Told by Two Sympathetic Observers*

Who Seek to Build Morals on a Foundation of Ruined Hopes. Berkeley, CA: University of California Press.

Price, David E. 1971. "Professionals and 'Entrepreneurs': Staff Orientations and Policymaking on Three Separate Committees." *Journal of Politics* 33: 316–36.

———. 1991. "Comment." In William H. Robinson and Clay Wellborn, eds., *Knowledge, Power and the Congress*, 128. Washington, DC: CQ Press.

Quirk, Paul J. 2005. "Deliberation and Decision Making." In Paul J. Quirk and Sarah A. Binder, eds., *The Legislative Branch*, 314–48. New York: Oxford University Press.

Quirk, Paul J., and William Bendix. 2011. "Deliberation in Congress." In Eric Schickler, Frances E. Lee, and George C. Edwards, eds., *The Oxford Handbook of the American Congress.* New York: Oxford University Press.

Quirk, Paul J., and Sarah A. Binder, eds. 2005. *The Legislative Branch.* New York: Oxford University Press.

Radin, Beryl A. 2000. *Beyond Machiavelli: Policy Analysis Comes of Age.* Washington, DC: Georgetown University Press.

Rieselbach, Leroy N. 1994. *Congressional Reform: The Changing Modern Congress.* Washington, DC: CQ Press.

Sabatier, Paul A. 1991. "Toward Better Theories of the Policy Process." *PS: Political Science and Politics* 24 (June): 147–56.

Schick, Allen. 1976. "The Supply and Demand for Policy Analysis on Capitol Hill." *Policy Analysis* 2 (Spring): 215–34.

Schickler, Eric. 2001. *Disjointed Pluralism: Institutional Innovation and the Development of the U.S. Congress.* Princeton, NJ: Princeton University Press.

Schickler, Eric, Frances E. Lee, and George C. Edwards, eds. 2011. *The Oxford Handbook of the American Congress.* New York: Oxford University Press.

Schuck, Peter H. 2014. *Why Government Fails So Often and How It Can Do Better.* Princeton, NJ: Princeton University Press.

Shepsle, Kenneth A. 1988. "Representation and Governance: The Great Legislative Trade-off." *Political Science Quarterly* 103: 461–84.

————. 1992. "Congress Is a 'They,' Not an 'It': Legislative Intent as Oxymoron." *International Review of Law and Economics* 12: 239–56.

Shipan, Charles R., and Craig Volden. 2012. "Policy Diffusion: Seven Lessons for Scholars and Practitioners." *Public Administration Review* 72 (November–December): 782–96.

Shulock, Nancy. 1999. "The Paradox of Policy Analysis: If It Is Not Used, Why Do We Produce So Much of It." *Journal of Policy Analysis and Management* 18: 226–44.

Skocpol, Theda. 1996. *Boomerang: Clinton's Health Security Effort and the Turn against Government in U.S. Politics.* New York: Norton.

Stokey, Edith, and Richard J. Zeckhauser. 1978. *A Primer for Policy Analysis.* New York: HarperCollins.

Stone, Deborah. 2001. *Policy Paradox: The Art of Political Decision Making.* 3rd ed. New York: Norton.

Sundquist, James L. 1981. *The Decline and Resurgence of Congress.* Washington, DC: Brookings Institution Press.

Sunstein, Cass. 1988. "Beyond the Republican Revival." *Yale Law Journal* 97: 1539–90.

Taylor, Andrew J. 2013. *Congress: A Performance Appraisal.* Boulder, CO: Westview Press.

VanDoren, Peter. 1989. "Should Congress Listen to Economists?" *Journal of Politics* 51 (May): 319–36.

Verdier, James M. 1984. "Advising Congressional Decision-Makers: Guidelines for Economists." *Journal of Policy Analysis and Management* 3: 421–38.

Vining, Aidan R., and David L. Weimer. 2006. "Efficiency and Cost-Benefit Analysis." In B. Guy Peters and Jon Pierre, eds., *Handbook of Public Policy*, 417–32. Thousand Oaks, CA: Sage.

————. 2010. "Policy Analysis," Foundations of Public Administration Series. www.aspanet.org/scriptcontent/index_par_foundationsseries.cfm.

Weaver, R. Kent. 2000. *Ending Welfare as We Know It.* Washington, D.C.: Brookings Institution Press.

Weimer, David L., and Aidan R. Vining. 1999. *Policy Analysis: Concepts and Practice.* 3rd ed. New York: Prentice Hall.

Weiss, Carol H. 1989. "Congressional Committees as Users of Analysis." *Journal of Policy Analysis and Management* 8: 411–31.

Whiteman, David. 1985. "The Fate of Policy Analysis in Congressional Decision Making: Three Types of Use in Committees." *Western Political Quarterly* 38 (June): 294–311.

Wildavsky, Aaron. 1979. *Speaking Truth to Power: The Art and Craft of Policy Analysis.* Boston, MA: Little, Brown.

Wilson, Woodrow. 1887. "The Study of Administration." *Political Science Quarterly* 2: 197–222.

Wolfinger, Raymond E. 1991. "Voter Turnout." *Society* 28: 23–26.

Wright, John R. 2003. *Interest Groups and Congress: Lobbying, Contributions, and Influence.* New York: Longman.

Zaller, John. 1992. *The Nature and Origins of Mass Opinion.* New York: Cambridge University Press.

Zelizer, Julian E. 1998. *Taxing America: Wilbur Mills, Congress, and the State, 1945–1975.* New York: Cambridge University Press.

CHAPTER FOUR

The Complicated and the Complex

Policy Analysis in an Era of Design

M. SUZANNE DONOVAN

Is policy analysis effective? The question begs clarification of the purpose of policy analysis. I would argue that it is to inform and advise decision makers (both policy makers and those who elect them) in order to improve the effectiveness of public policy. It generally does so by

1. clarifying the nature of a social problem;
2. identifying potential solutions and predicting their impacts; and/or
3. evaluating the effectiveness or consequences of a policy after it has been implemented in order to inform future decisions.

The purpose of policy analysis is distinct from policy advocacy, which is intended from its start to change the priority attached to

With thanks to Allie Huyghe for her excellent research assistance.

a problem, shape values and beliefs, and promote predetermined solutions. Yet the line between analysis and advocacy can become blurred since analysts, too, have values and beliefs. Eugene Bardach (2011) proposes an eightfold path to steer the policy professional to consideration of relevant analytic concepts before he or she proposes a policy solution. But values and beliefs can be introduced at the very point of departure down the path: defining the problem. The disciplines in which the policy analyst is trained provide a set of lenses through which problems can be viewed and a set of tools with which potential solutions can be constructed. The way one defines or frames a problem—the disciplinary lens chosen and the implications for the solution that the choice entails—may elevate particular values and promote solutions that are predictable if not predetermined.

While claims to neutrality may be contested, policy analysis has nonetheless contributed to policy debates that have led to major changes in how we live: in the amount of energy we consume and the number of solar panels individuals choose to install, in the level of pollution to which we are exposed and the number of plastic bags that get tossed to the wind. It has informed policy decisions regarding the floor for workers' compensation provided by the minimum wage and the earned income tax credit and alternative approaches to keeping Social Security solvent. The model underlying policy analyses in each of these cases is the remarkably powerful market model. By the relatively simple act of offering a positive incentive through tax breaks or higher wages, or by providing a negative incentive through a charge or a penalty for noncompliance, policy makers have had significant and far-reaching impacts on personal and business decisions.

But there are arenas in which policy analysis has been far less successful. Perhaps because economic models are so powerful in some circumstances, policy analysts at times overuse them or have blind spots in applying them. This chapter explores two such blind spots. The first is application of the economic model when critical underlying assumptions of the model do not hold. The second involves system complexity; the greater the dependence of actors in the system targeted for change on the decisions of others to produce a desired outcome, the weaker will be the impact of incentive and accountability mechanisms. Policy analyses and recommendations aimed at improving K–12 education, the focus of this chapter, have suffered from both of these shortcomings.

The central arguments in the chapter do not apply to education policy alone; there are parallels in other policy arenas in which government seeks to influence the quality of services delivered in complex environments, including medical care, welfare, and employment training. The focus on education is a function of familiarity; the arguments presented rest more on accumulated experience working at the intersections of education policy, practice, research, and design than on the scholarly research literature. Herbert Simon reflected on these same issues decades ago in *The Sciences of the Artificial* ([1969] 1996), arguing that the design challenges described here are relevant to all professional practice, and I draw on his thinking as well. The chapter concludes with suggestions for revising Bardach's eightfold path and expanding the tools of policy analysis.

EDUCATION POLICY: THE FAILURE OF GOOD IDEAS

Few would contest that improving K–12 public education in the United States is a high-priority policy problem. Students in the

United States are routinely outperformed on international tests not only by other countries with similar histories of development, but by some newly developed countries as well (Economist Intelligence Unit 2014). The dropout rate is high by any measure (Heckman and LaFontaine 2010), and those who complete high school often require remedial courses in college (Bettinger and Long 2009). The achievement gap between students whose families are at the high and low ends of the income distribution is more pronounced in the United States than in most other developed countries (OECD 2012), and the gap continues to widen (Kirsch and Braun 2016).

Stating the high-level problem is straightforward, but it is not yet represented in a solvable way. Bardach (2011: 2) suggests that, for any policy problem, "it is usually helpful to view the situation through the 'market failure' lens." If there is no market failure identified, he warns, it is very difficult to find solutions to problems—at least solutions that do not bring many adverse side effects. At the same time, Bardach acknowledges that there are a few exceptions, including "failure of government to function well in areas in which it is traditionally expected to act effectively (e.g., in providing public schools)" (3). That the delivery of education service may fall into a different category of problem appears to be overlooked by many scholars and policy analysts.

Market failures, which abound in education, have been a persistent focus of policy analysts (Hanushek and Lindseth 2009). Wages of teachers are rarely tied to performance. Families often have highly constrained choices, blunting competition's disciplining influence on quality. There are, at best, weak mechanisms for forcing failing public schools out of business.[1] And students often have too little incentive to achieve. The favored policy tools at both the federal and state levels, incentives and accountability, reflect the market failure framing of the problem (Hannaway and Woodroffe 2003): Teachers should be evaluated and paid for performance (Podgursky and Springer 2007), and parents should be given choice among public schools (Betts and Loveless 2005; Hoxby 2003) or supported with vouchers to go to independent or parochial schools (Chubb and Mo 1990). In some cases, paying students for performance has been proposed and tested (Fryer 2010a). Federal incentives have been directed at the state and district level to reward policy changes with additional resources (ARRA 2009).

The federal government does invest in education research and development intended to improve the quality of the education system, though the sums are paltry—less than half a billion dollars annually, compared to thirty billion in medicine (AAAS 2014). From the economist's perspective, how students learn and how teachers teach is not factored into the equation. This is not because it is considered irrelevant but because it is relegated to a black box: it is assumed to be a level of detail that does not require attention in order to effect change. The ability to leave the black box unopened is precisely what makes policies that improve the functioning of markets appealing. When we provide a tax incentive to purchase a hybrid vehicle, we do not need to know about the thought processes or calculations individuals make regarding their purchase decision.[2] It is enough to know that for a particular incentive, we can expect aggregate behavior to change by an estimated amount. Consumer decisions can be complicated of course, and people in Detroit may respond differently from people in California to the same incentive. But we can predict the direction of the effect and can gather evidence to get a respectable estimate of impact. Nor do we need to be concerned about the processes automakers use to decide on the number of hybrids to produce since market forces will move toward equilibrium. In cases such as this, relegating thought processes to a black box is extremely efficient. Advertising agents who serve auto companies may need to understand what goes on in consumers' heads; thankfully the policy analyst does not.

Incentives work to change behavior when people have the capacity but not the impetus to behave in the desired way. But if capacity is a barrier, if people do not know how to do what they are incentivized to do, then incentives will not produce the desired improvement. This may explain the outcome reported when students in Washington, DC, were given a monetary incentive to improve their behavior (including showing up at school on time and in uniform) and for academic performance. Students changed the behaviors that were straightforward and easily defined. But improving academic performance—which required that students know how to improve—did not significantly change (Fryer 2010b).

When the problem is one of capacity, investment is required—a response that is itself entirely consistent with economic theory. But to know what investments will be productive, the black box must be opened in order to understand where the weaknesses in capacity lie and what changes will generate the necessary capacity. In the case of education, what goes on inside the school system and the classroom, and the cognitive processes inside the heads of teachers, students, and administrators, moves into the arena of interest.

Inside the Black Box

In 1999 the National Research Council (NRC) published a study synthesizing research on how people learn (Bransford, Brown,

Figure 8. Illustration in *Fish Is Fish* by Leo Lionni. Reprinted from Lionni 1987 with permission from Penguin Random House LLC.

and Cocking 1999). The U.S. Department of Education commissioned the study because it too was interested in prying open the black box. The study is relevant here for one of its central points, a point demonstrated most efficiently by a children's story told by Leo Lionni (1987) and recounted in the NRC report. In the story, a tadpole grows legs and, unlike his friend the fish, is able to explore on land. He comes back and reports to the fish what he saw. With accurate descriptions of the characteristics of a bird, a cow, and a human, the fish pictures the images in figure 8.

The story captures poignantly what a now-extensive body of research demonstrates: students understand the world primarily through their everyday experiences. The human brain is a sense-making machine that has been actively at work long before a child reaches preschool (Shonkoff and Phillips 2000). If new knowledge is not to be flimsily tacked on to everyday experience, students' existing conceptions must be drawn out and reshaped; their misconceptions must be actively dislodged. For this reason, learning for understanding (as distinct from acquisition of information—which the fish managed quite well) is less likely to happen if the teacher does the talking and students are silent and passive. Yet this is the model that dominates K–12 education (Applebee et al. 2003). The more limited the student's exposure outside of schools, the greater will be the gap between everyday experience and the desired goal state. The logical conclusion is that if our goal is for all students to learn for understanding, then the primary approach to teaching in U.S. schools is misguided.

When the *How People Learn* report was finished, the Department of Education asked, If this is what we know about human learning, what does it tell us about improving K–12 education? After convening a panel of education practitioners and a panel of policy makers, the answer offered in a second NRC report was, succinctly paraphrased, *not much*. The report concluded that a more encouraging response would require that the research knowledge be elaborated in formats and at a level of detail that is useful for practitioners and policy makers, that research targeted at improving practice would need to involve teams that combine the expertise of researchers with that of education practitioners, and that learning research would need to include more intensive study of classroom practice (Donovan, Bransford, and Pellegrino 1999: 3). What the report did not say, but what can be extrapolated from its findings, was that incentives and accountability as policy tools will have limited impact because the knowledge and tools required to better educate the nation's children either are not widely accessible or do not exist at all.

In a series of NRC reports that followed, we organized knowledge in frameworks intended to clarify implications for policy and practice: with respect to the teaching and learning of history, mathematics, and science (Donovan and Bransford 2005), with respect to preschool education (Bowman, Donovan, and Burns 2000), and with respect to the assignment of minority students to special and gifted education (Donovan and Cross 2002). Such efforts continue at the NRC today. But synthesizing knowledge and changing practice are quite different enterprises, even when the synthesis is accompanied by policy recommendations.

Building an Organizational Infrastructure

Many sectors share the challenge of bridging research and practice, and yet in medicine, agriculture, and transportation, scientific research has fueled major change in a way that we do not see in public education. Bruce Alberts, president of the National Academy of Sciences from 1993 to 2005, commissioned two National Research Council panels to explore the contributors to this discrepancy. What was learned from experts in these other sectors is that the knowledge and tools that shape and reshape practice generally have their roots not in laboratories but in practice settings (Donovan, Wigdor, and Snow 2003). Theory emerges from the observation of the unexpected, interventions are tested in the contexts in which they must operate, and relationships of trust are built through shared purpose and routine contact. In medicine the federal government supports teaching hospitals and academic medical centers where research and practice comingle, and it supports agricultural extension stations where, as one agricultural expert explained, researchers hang over the fence with farmers, metaphorically planting the seeds for changes in practice. But education researchers have no practice settings in which they routinely engage in research and development, though the medical and agricultural comparisons suggest that such an infrastructure can be supported at scale.

Richard Elmore argued decades ago that the further removed the actions to be influenced are from policy makers and the more intermediaries who come between, the less effective will be top-down policy initiatives (Elmore 1979). He argued that policy in these cases should begin at ground level and be mapped backwards in order to be responsive to the context in which change is to occur. The NRC committee proposed the creation of a new institution whose mission would be to establish *field sites*—schools and districts in which researchers, practitioners, and education designers would interact routinely in the settings where the change in practice would ultimately occur. The role of public policy envisioned by the committee was not to provide incentives or establish accountability but to invest in infrastructure for problem solving in context. The envisioned research and development programs to be conducted in field sites were to draw on the expertise of university researchers in the variety of disciplines that contribute to the knowledge for improving education practice. The research teams would be linked through networks of individuals working on similar problems in different sites, and a national organization would be responsible for accumulating knowledge and creating coherence.

In 2003, with a small grant from the National Academy of Sciences, the Strategic Education Research Partnership (SERP) was created as that independent entity. The NRC committee argued that to launch the enterprise would require $500 million in the first five to seven years. Policy makers looking for silver bullets—for the simple lever that can be pulled with the promise of quick impact on student achievement—did not see the appeal. Investing in an infrastructure for the ongoing generation of knowledge and tools to improve education practice did not have the ring of a flying bullet.

With private funds initially, supplemented eventually with federal research grants for specific projects, the SERP enterprise was launched on a relatively small scale to determine the feasibility and productivity of an investment in the infrastructure to bring researchers and practitioners together on problems of educational practice. Evidence from more than a decade provides a proof of concept: organizing research and development around problems of practice, and conducting that work in collaboration with practitioners in practice settings, is indeed feasible, and it affects the usability of the knowledge for changing education practice (Donovan, Snow, and Daro 2013).

Designing for Complexity

Moving the improvement effort closer to the point of influence, as Elmore (1979) advocated, is necessary but not sufficient to have a positive impact on educational practice and outcomes. Public education falls into a class of difficult-to-solve problems Richard Nelson wrote about decades ago in his provocatively titled essay, *The Moon and the Ghetto* (1977). Nelson draws the distinction between problems such as sending a rocket to the moon, which can be solved because we know what it is we are trying to do and we have the expertise to do it, and problems like poverty or improving schooling for which we have no widely accepted description of the challenge, let alone potent approaches to solution (Nelson 2011).

In a similar vein, organizational psychologists and scholars of business management have distinguished between problems they place in the "complicated" category and those they categorize as "complex" (Glouberman and Zimmerman 2002; Kegan and Lahey

2009; Kurtz and Snowden 2003). Complicated problems such as the moon landing may require many steps that must be coordinated, but one can generate a blueprint for the work to be done. There may be failures in a complicated system, but the discrete nature of the tasks make it possible to identify a weak point, thus allowing for accountability. This is not to say that getting a shuttle to the moon is anything less than a major organizational feat; it is subject to human failure at every turn, as was so vividly demonstrated by the Mars orbiter disaster as a consequence of using the imperial system of measurement rather than the metric system (Pollack 1999). But the point is that we can identify why the system failed and who was responsible and fix it.

For complex problems, in contrast, there is no blueprint. The outcomes of interest emerge not from the sum of actions of many individuals but from unpredictable *interactions* among people. The unpredictability is not a function of inexplicability but of bounded rationality; of complexity beyond our ability to model (Simon 1996). K–12 education bears all the markers of complexity. One need only follow a class of students during a school day to observe the variation in the behavior and academic engagement of students across classes with different teachers. Troublemakers in one class can be focused students in another. While it is tempting to conclude that the issue is simply one of the teachers' expertise, one need only observe several classes of students with the same experienced teacher to question that conclusion. Even when the teacher teaches the same lesson across untracked classes at the same grade level, the ways in which the class of students responds often vary. The active interest of a popular student, for example, can change the dynamic of the entire lesson. And the same teacher who is considered excellent in one school context can struggle in another.

Complexity is also captured in the findings that collective efficacy—the belief among a team of professionals at a school that they are able to effectively educate students (Goddard 2001)—and relational trust (Bryk and Schneider 2002) among adults in a school have powerful impacts on teaching and learning.

Improving complex systems, whether K–12 public education, hospitals, or social service agencies, requires a different set of analytic tools than those typically found in the policy analyst's tool box. Policy analysts generally draw on research-based knowledge and evidence to identify and support a defensible approach to solving a problem. Once the desired policy is identified, the problem then becomes one of implementation. With respect to vaccinations, lead poisoning, and tax policy, this is a sensible approach. When intervening in complex social systems, however, there is generally less clarity about the precise nature of the problem, and implementation is by far the most daunting challenge. Questions regarding what people do and why—what they know and believe, when they engage or resist change, how they interact to get a task accomplished—belong not in the post-analysis implementation considerations but in the very center of the policy design process. Accomplishing policy goals requires a different mind-set and a different set of tools because the change in behavior that is sought cannot be clearly defined at the outset.

Can policy analysis be effective when the system targeted for improvement is so complex and our capacity for rationality is bounded? Or should policy analysts simply accept that the tools of the trade have their limitations and acknowledge that the pace of innovation will inevitably be uneven, as Richard Nelson (2011) would have us do)? Rejecting pessimism, Herbert Simon (1996) argues that while we may not be able to "solve" complex problems, or even see our way to an end goal, we can design for the problems in view. With each step forward we will have a new vantage point that will provide a broader view, and we can make progress so long as we design with the intention of keeping options open (Simon 1996: 156). SERP's work with school districts corroborates Simon's view. An example of precisely this is described below.

DESIGN FOR EDUCATIONAL IMPROVEMENT: A CASE EXAMPLE

A school district serving as a SERP field site nominated the downward slide in mathematics achievement in middle school as the focal problem. To understand the nature of the problem at its source, a team of researchers worked with teacher "co-developers."[3] The teachers were given small recorders and trained by researchers to do a think-aloud protocol in which individual students were given a problem and asked to verbalize their thinking as they worked toward a solution. To their surprise, teachers found that students—even those who performed well on math tests—rarely tried to make sense of situations in word problems, or to think through the nature of the question being posed. Rather, they began combining numbers in accordance with the procedures recently taught or in response to signals in the wording of a problem about the operation that was required. When probed further, students revealed that they did not think mathematics was supposed to make sense.

The goal of the SERP team, consistent with research that contrasts U.S. mathematics classrooms with Japanese classrooms (U.S. Department of Education 2003) and with the research summarized in the *How People Learn* report (Bransford, Brown, and Cocking 1999; Donovan, Bransford, and Pellegrino 1999), became one of shifting the culture of the classroom from answer getting to sense making: focusing teachers on students' reasoning, explanation, justification, and modeling of problems. The team designed for small changes in instructional practice that were then tried by teachers. Student reactions were reported, and work samples were brought back to the team. From the collaboration, a set of simple but potentially powerful "sense-making tools" were crafted (http://math.serpmedia.org /sense-making/).

An example of one technique appears in figure 9. Any word problem can be broken into three parts: the stem or problem situation, the question, and the solution. Students are generally given the stem and the question and must find the solution. Teachers were encouraged instead to vary the part that students were given. Sometimes students would be given only the stem, and they had to provide the questions that could be answered with the information given. If a student is only told that a dragonfly flies fifty feet in two seconds and is asked to formulate questions that can be answered with that information, he or she must think about the meaning of the two quantities and the relationship between them. A second technique was to give students the solution and ask that they write their own problem stem for which that solution would hold. Many students found the situation generation appealing; though it is a much more cognitively demanding task, it gave them permission to create scenarios such as sharks eating people at the beach at a particular rate.

The techniques were beautiful in their simplicity and supported the targeted shift in student behavior. But challenges soon surfaced:

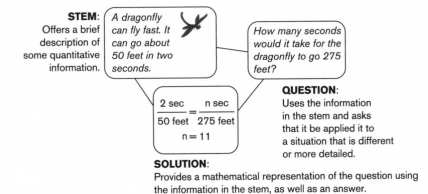

STEM: Offers a brief description of some quantitative information.

A dragonfly can fly fast. It can go about 50 feet in two seconds.

How many seconds would it take for the dragonfly to go 275 feet?

$$\frac{2 \text{ sec}}{50 \text{ feet}} = \frac{n \text{ sec}}{275 \text{ feet}}$$
$$n = 11$$

QUESTION: Uses the information in the stem and asks that it be applied it to a situation that is different or more detailed.

SOLUTION: Provides a mathematical representation of the question using the information in the stem, as well as an answer.

Figure 9. STEM-QUESTION-SOLUTION Triangles.

1) When teachers successfully shift the focus of the classroom toward student reasoning, students typically reveal that they are using below-grade-level mathematics to solve problems. Teachers often find this acceptable because lower-level mathematics can produce the right answer to the problem in many cases (e.g., repeated addition can get the same answer as multiplication), and the consequences of not learning the grade-level mathematics often do not show up until students move into the next grade. Mathematics teachers' frustration with the poor prior preparation of students is rampant.

2) When students' reasoning is at the center of the instructional activity, a major source of unpredictability is introduced into a lesson. Teachers often are unsure what to do with what students say. Pedagogical content knowledge is often too weak to allow teachers to use divergent thinking among students as a resource for learning.

Without careful structuring of a lesson, teachers become anxious that spending time listening to student thinking is not preparing students for success on accountability tests. Without the knowledge of how to use student reasoning to consolidate understanding of grade-level mathematics, teachers justifiably conclude that too little learning is happening. Even the teacher co-developers reverted to more familiar approaches to instruction when they were not engaged in the research-related activities.

We abandoned the idea that the minimally invasive sense-making techniques could by themselves accomplish our goal. We incorporated those techniques into a set of fully designed "Poster Problem" lessons.[4] To address the challenge of inadequate teacher knowledge regarding the mathematical point of the lesson, each problem was accompanied by "teacher tune-ups" that clearly specify the mathematical target of the lesson (http://math.serpmedia .org/poster_problems/teacher-tune-ups.html). In order to prepare teachers for the unpredictability of what students will say and do, the teacher supports for the lesson provide examples of a range of student work and an explanation of the important distinctions among those work examples. While students' thinking may appear to be wildly unpredictable, it can generally be sorted by major features into just a few categories. Teachers' uncertainty regarding what students will say and do can thus be reduced and their confidence bolstered. Furthermore, teacher supports include the ordering of students' thinking about the problem solution on a progression: from misguided or incorrect through correct but inefficient or below grade level to effective use of the targeted grade-level mathematics. Teachers are then given guidance about using the variation in thinking to move all students to grade-level mathematics.

While it is tempting to elaborate further on the many features of the Poster Problems lesson design that attend to both the research knowledge base and the demonstrated needs of teachers, for present purposes it is more relevant that the approach to crafting the lessons explicitly incorporated principles of *user-centered design* (d. school 2010). As a problem-solving technique, user-centered design removes the primary motivations of the people whose behavior is targeted for change from a black box and elevates them to a central role in the design of solutions. Through an "empathy" process that requires questioning and careful listening on the part of those designing solutions, experiences, constraints, goals, and beliefs are uncovered that shape the specifications for a solution. This is not to say that the goals of the user trump the goals of the policy maker/client (in this case, the school district). Rather, the assumption is that in a complex system in which outcomes cannot be assigned to the actions of individuals, accomplishing the policy maker's goal is more likely if the design of a solution takes into account the goals of the end user. Instead of determining policy solutions at a distance and relegating failure to create the desired change in behavior to an implementation challenge, user-centered design attends to those whose behavior is targeted for change from the start.

The Poster Problems are not by themselves a solution to the problem of ineffective instruction in middle grades mathematics, nor should we expect them to be. They are designed both to support student learning and to respond to the needs of teachers, but teachers operate inside a complex organization. As Simon (1996) suggested, addressing one problem in a complex system creates a vantage point from which the next layer of the problem can be viewed and understood.

Following the Contours of the Problem

The mathematics work confronted us with yet another challenge we had not anticipated when we began working on what the partnership team believed to be primarily a classroom-level problem. Though it is patently obvious that classrooms exist within schools and schools exist within districts, the extent to which classroom-level change requires solutions to problems elsewhere in the system was not initially appreciated. Of most immediate importance, teachers are given feedback and are evaluated by principals. And principals bring expectations regarding quality instruction when they observe in classrooms. A classroom in which students are actively engaged in sense-making looks very different from a traditional classroom. In the best classrooms students are given time to revise their thinking with patient prodding from the teacher. When teachers work with student thinking, lessons may at times appear to go more slowly in the sense that fewer problems are "covered." And when students solve problems in groups, the classroom becomes noisy. Productive engagement may appear to the untrained eye as sanctioned chaos.

To address this problem, we began a second user-centered design process, this time with principals as the target. Our goal was to change the principals' preferences with regard to instruction—the attributes they look for when they observe in classrooms. The empathy process revealed that while principals feel responsible for serving as instructional leaders, the volume of leadership and administrative tasks and the necessity of working with teachers across all content areas leave them with little time to learn. They were not averse to change; they were averse to the process they are generally put through in efforts to change them. They wanted no transformative experiences accompanied by thick binders of reading materials filled with aspirations and goals that—even when they are compelling—seem only loosely related to their day-to-day work. If we wanted to change their preferences, we would need to respond to their demand for concrete approaches that required as little reading as possible.

The product of the user-centered design process was what we refer to as the "5x8 card" (math.serpmedia.org/5x8card). The card is named for its size to acknowledge the design constraints of the principals; the amount of text they would be asked to digest would fit within a 5-inch by 8-inch space. Through a rapid prototyping process (d. school 2010) in collaboration with two school districts, the card's content became a set of seven "student vital actions" that are easy to observe. One vital action is, "Students say a second sentence (spontaneously or prompted by the teacher or another student) to explain their thinking and connect it to their first sentence." In typical math classrooms, students speak single sentences or phrases, if they speak at all, generally to supply an answer or ask a clarifying question. If a student is speaking a second sentence connected by logic, he or she is explaining in some way: giving a reason, an example, a qualification, or a source of evidence. A principal can quickly and easily see whether a classroom is one in which there are many, few, or no second sentences. Use of the card allows principals to become more focused when they visit classrooms and to develop a preference for the shift in practice we sought to create. While the approach requires little learning up front, principals can learn a great deal over time as they become more expert at identifying the vital actions and the associated characteristics of the classrooms in which they are and are not present.

The principals with whom we worked embraced the 5x8 card, appreciating its simplicity. But the challenge does not end there.

Principals, too, have supervisors whose expectations and priorities will either support a sustained focus on the part of principals or draw attention elsewhere. Classroom change is, ultimately, a systems challenge. But because those in the system typically see only their own piece, change requires the design of tools that can allow for coordination and coherence across those pieces. These include "boundary objects" that allow people in different parts of the system to focus and work together on a shared goal (Benson et al. 2012; Coburn 2003; Star and Griesemer 1989).

Addressing the systemic nature of the problem requires aligning the actions of all those who must be supportive of a change so that obstacles to success—competing priorities, failures of communication, scheduling conflicts—can be successfully addressed. The many ways in which a system acts to reject or undermine an intervention must itself be treated as a set of problems to be solved (Stein and Coburn 2008).

IMPLICATIONS FOR POLICY ANALYSIS

In the decade since the NRC's SERP report was released, policy discussions and decisions at the federal and state levels have focused on accountability standards, incentives for evaluation of teacher performance, support for charter schools, and incentives for students. Some have celebrated the fading of the political divide: both Republicans and Democrats are supporting incentives and accountability as the major policy solutions (Maranto and McShane 2012). Investment in the capacity of educators and in the research and development located in practice settings that is essential for developing the tools for improvement has been minuscule by comparison.

As a consequence not only have we seen the failure to achieve intended policy goals on a large scale,[5] but in some respects the effects have been negative. Accountability standards incentivized by the bipartisan No Child Left Behind (NCLB) legislation, for example, were intended to ensure that students at the bottom of the achievement ladder—those from disadvantaged backgrounds or with special needs—were given the necessary instructional attention to support their success. Given the absence of capacity for improvement and the complexity of introducing change in the public education system, the policy not only fell short of its goal, but led to a reduction or elimination of science education, art education, and physical education in many schools, most notably those with the highest concentration of disadvantaged students (Cawelti 2006; Griffith and Scharmann 2008). And preparing for accountability testing may itself be undermining learning. In a recent survey of teachers in two school districts involved in a SERP literacy project, preparation for accountability tests was cited by 70 percent of teachers as the most important factor preventing implementation of the instructional program.[6]

The reactions of school systems to NCLB cannot be excused as an unintended consequence of an otherwise sound policy; the very logic of the policy is fundamentally flawed both because there is a major capacity problem (NCEE 2015) and because the systems targeted for improvement are complex. For these reasons we should have expected that a firmer push for accountability would

- undermine collective efficacy in an effort to hold individuals accountable;
- promote the exodus of teachers and administrators who are frustrated with expectations they cannot meet,

particularly from schools in which classroom behavioral challenges are greatest and school organization is weakest; and

· distort instructional decisions by gaming for high scores rather than aiming for genuine learning.

We may very well repeat the mistakes of NCLB with the push for College and Career Ready Standards (including the Common Core State Standards and the Next Generation Science Standards). The standards are more targeted at critical conceptual understanding in response to criticism of earlier standards. They incorporate practice standards that promote argumentation and discussion—known contributors to deeper learning (Lawrence and Snow 2010; Murphy et al. 2009). But the capacity to reach the new standards does not now exist. And if we fail to invest in and design for the systemic capacity building that will be required to shift practice, we should not hold high hopes for improvement.

Carol Weiss (1982) argued that policy analysis has a subtle impact over the long run because the ideas it introduces seep bit by bit into the thinking of government analysts and policy makers. There can be little doubt that incentives and accountability have seeped to a point of saturation. Their appeal to policy makers subject to the ticking clock of election cycles is perhaps inevitable; investing in capacity and designing for improvement in education systems takes longer and comes with a higher price tag. But it is the job of the policy analyst to frame the problem, inform the debate, and predict the consequences of alternative policies. And policy analysts too have relied heavily on incentives and accountability as the primary strategies (Hannaway and Woodroffe 2003).

When so many important social problems reside in the operation of complex systems, why have we not seen greater attention in policy analyses to the challenges of designing for improvement of those systems? Simon (1996: 112) argues that professional schools, in a bid for status in the university community, have largely abdicated responsibility for teaching design: "In terms of the prevailing norms, academic respectability calls for subject matter that is intellectually tough, analytic, formalizable, and teachable." The concession to the professional training function, he argues, is to attach the word *applied* to a respected field, such as "applied economics." But professional schools in his view can only prepare their students for complex social design challenges if social design is a central subject of study. "Whether we have the formal tools we need or not," he writes, "the topics are too crucial to the social design process to permit them to be ignored or omitted from the curriculum" (166).

All public policy is social design, of course. But the extent to which policy analysts are trained in design is quite limited. Bardach's eightfold path, for example, suggests that the analyst look for solutions others have already found to solving the problem at hand. He acknowledges that there may be times when the analyst must design a solution, and he offers some guidance in this regard: "Design problems usually have two stages. These stages are (1) design the system as it is projected to run in its steady state, and (2) plan the strategy of change that would take us from here to there. The first stage is predominantly technical; the second, predominantly political and bureaucratic" (Bardach 2011: 28). This conception of design is substantially different from one that concedes at the start that the end state cannot be projected; that what is possible must be revealed over time through efforts to understand the system by understanding those who comprise it, and how their purposes and behaviors can be changed through design efforts.

Broadening the Eightfold Path

If policy analysis has been less effective with complex problems such as public education, how might it be improved? I offer three suggestions.

I. EXPLORE THE CHALLENGES OF PROBLEM REPRESENTATION MORE DEEPLY. Simon (1996: 129) argues that "solving a problem simply means representing it so as to make the solution transparent" and adds, "a deeper understanding of how representations are created and how they contribute to the solution of problems will become an essential component in the future theory of design." Until such a theory of design is in hand, perhaps a more modest change might be made to the eightfold path's first step: Define the Problem. Bardach suggests that the analyst begin by considering whether there is a market failure. A first improvement might be to add the explicit consideration of whether the capacity for change is present. The answer will determine whether incentives (positive or negative) are viable solutions.

The second question I would nominate for explicit attention in Step 1 is whether the problem of concern is simple, complicated, or complex. In the latter case, attention to the ramifications of complexity must be paid on the entire journey down the eightfold path, particularly when designing alternative solutions. For simple or complicated problems, the policy analyst can be clear about the goal state and propose paths to achieve it from a distance using technical knowledge, expertise, and information, as Bardach suggests. As argued above, for complex problems identifying the goal from a distance and developing plans to achieve that goal is likely to be a fool's errand. Policy to effectively address complex problems from a distance is likely to be limited to investments in the structures and capacity for continuous improvement efforts in close proximity to practice. For the most part, however, the policy considerations are so significantly different when a problem resides in a complex system that perhaps a fork in the eightfold path is warranted. The specifics of the operations of the system to be influenced, and the goals, motivations, and behaviors of those inside the system, must be the starting point for design rather than post-design implementation concerns.

2. TEACH USER-CENTERED DESIGN SKILLS. While there may be no science of design, Simon urges us to see the creation of one as a necessity for the effective preparation of professionals.[7] Stanford University is noteworthy in having created a design school, the Hasso Plattner Institute of Design, where user-centered design is taught to those in professional schools throughout the university (d. school 2010). But if analysts who advise superintendents, school boards, governors, and federal policy makers, and who populate state and district offices and nonprofit organizations, are to have the tools for recognizing and tackling complex problems, user-centered design skills would serve them well, thus warranting a place in the public policy curriculum.

It is no doubt a difficult case to make that a process centered on "empathy" for the user is appropriate university training given the divide that is often assumed between the emotional (with which empathy is generally associated) and the rational. In an important respect, however, the empathy process is empirically quite rigorous, perhaps more than the imposition of an economics framework, with its embedded assumptions about what motivates the behavior of individuals. When what one is trying to understand and influence is decision making in the marketplace, equating utility maximization with monetary incentives is generally a practice that is sound enough for many policy purposes. It captures activity on the scale of interest (even if some percentage of individuals behave differently from the assumed behavior). In complex systems in which individuals have only weak control over outcomes that involve the interaction of many, assumptions made from a distance about individuals' motivations are likely to have less predictive validity.

Introducing user-centered design as a tool for policy analysts risks little; if the behaviors policy makers seek to influence are indeed motivated by the individual pursuit of monetary benefit, empathy processes will reveal as much. But in today's world in which the interactions among people are rapidly changing, in which big data allow for a far more nuanced view of behavior, in which people form virtual communities, share resources freely, and provide each other with information and support on a larger scale than was ever before possible, it is perhaps a healthy discipline to deploy methods that subject policy analysts' assumptions about behavior to a reality check.

3. EXPAND EXPOSURE TO SYSTEMS THINKING AND IMPROVEMENT SCIENCE. Systems thinking is at the heart of every scientific discipline. The economy, governments, the body, and the universe are all systems. But in the shift from *understanding* how things work to *changing* how things work, we often lose sight of the very system we are trying to improve. Bardach (2011) encourages

analysts to model the system as part of designing solutions. But complex systems may be challenging to map, and in some cases feasible only through iterative efforts to improve the system. Those in a complex system may not themselves have a clear understanding of the system's functioning. Constraints or weaknesses in the system may only be revealed by bumping up against them. After engaging in improvement efforts with school systems, for example, we observed parallel lines of influence leading to the classroom with little communication across them; weak or no feedback lines that flow from those expected to enact policies in the classroom to those setting the policies; and weak mechanisms at best for distilling and documenting what is learned and for preserving knowledge in the system.

By following the contours of problems of practice in the mathematics case described above, we broadened our focus step by step until mapping the system became our explicit goal. Donald Berwick, founder of the Institute for Healthcare Improvement, describes a similar process of learning to see the health care system through attempts to improve it (Berwick 2008). Policy analysts may be better prepared to see the system, and thus more efficient, if their training includes the explicit study of systems, with attention to such features as the homeostatic mechanisms that give systems stability in a changing environment, points in the system that are more and less permeable, paths along which information travels through the system, where retrospective feedback is received and how it is processed, and where and how knowledge is documented, managed, and preserved in the system.

In the field of health care and in industry more generally, a "science of improvement" has emerged to support more systematic and systemic approaches to improving the performance of complex systems (Berwick 2008; Langley et al. 2009). Whether it can legitimately be called a science (given that its task is more akin to engineering) need not be resolved in order to see its value. The tools provide a structure for mapping the system, identifying the key drivers of change, and attending to obstacles as they emerge. They are useful in guiding the change process—in calling attention to the challenges for which design of materials and tools is required, as well as those that require agreement or coordination (Donovan 2013).

Continuous improvement processes hold promise for the complex problems like education for which policy has been largely ineffective (Bryk et al. 2015). But those processes require the development of knowledge management systems and improvement structures, and schools systems currently have neither. Policy decisions would need to be made to allocate resources for this purpose, an unlikely outcome unless policy analysts appreciate their affordances and give them a place commensurate with incentives and accountability in their recommendations.

LOOKING FORWARD

When they were established as distinct entities half a century ago, public policy schools were intended to provide interdisciplinary training. But they also pushed on the analytic frameworks of the disciplines, asking that economists impose on themselves a concern for unintended consequences, that political scientists see the power not only of the visible hand of legislators in taking action but also of the invisible hand that thwarts or promotes the effectiveness of those actions, and that lawyers consider not only what the law can prevent from happening but also the positive role it can play in shaping social policy.

Half a century later, perhaps it is time to ask what frameworks and tools the policy analyst needs for the decades ahead. The pace of change in human behavior has been breathtaking. Entrepreneurs recognized what could be changed, and through user-centered design made us want to change. They made it possible for those of us who knew little about computer technology to navigate by using icons with familiar images, and to learn what we need to learn as we need to learn it. Rather than require that we share their purpose, they designed for each of us to use the devices for our own purposes—to do as much or as little with them as our varied interests would have us do. Much like the principals who were willing to embrace change if it allowed them to learn as they go rather than requiring extensive reading, we learn and become more adept with our technology as we use it.

Not only is designing for those whose behavior we intend to change essential when we are dealing with complex systems in which both incentives and accountability are weak instruments; it can improve policy outcomes even for simple problems. While a five cent charge for a disposable grocery bag attaches a price to an externality, how many of us conserve instead because a sturdy cloth bag that rolls into a fist-size ball for portability adds an element of convenience? How does it affect our feelings about ourselves and others when we see that we are collectively able to change an aspect of our everyday behavior for the good of society and of the planet? And what are the recursive effects beyond grocery store bags as a consequence of those feelings?

Bardach (2011: xvi) opens his guide to policy analysis with the claim that "policy analysis is more art than science." I would replace the word *art* with *design*. Design certainly has artistic components, but it can be subjected to principled and empirical study that can lead to predictions about the kinds of policies that will be effective in a way that art cannot. After fifty years of training policy analysts who have done far better with complicated problems than complex problems, perhaps it is time to reconsider Simon's call for professional schools to elevate design to a more central role.

NOTES

1. No Child Left Behind requires that schools be "restructured" if they have failed to make adequate yearly progress for five consecutive years.

2. I do not intend to slight the important contributions of behavioral economics, which tries to understand common cognitive limitations that cause many people to make decisions that would not be expected by the traditional economic model of utility maximization. See, e.g., McCaffery and Slemrod 2006. I am referring instead to the analytic practice of using a model of decision making that is assumed to apply to the whole population under study, rather than learning about decision processes in all their variety.

3. This research was led by Alan Schoenfeld, Elizabeth and Edward Conner Professor of Education and Affiliated Professor of Mathematics, University of California, Berkeley; and Phil Daro, Bay Area Math Director, SERP Institute.

4. The name reflects the concept proposed by teachers that the problems could be chosen to vividly serve as the poster child for an important mathematical idea. Teachers could then easily refer back to the idea via the vivid image of slicing cheese or mixing chocolate milk. This work was led by Matthew Ellinger, Director of Media and Design, SERP Institute.

5. This is not to say that there have been no beneficiaries of the policies or pockets of improvement as a consequence, but rather that the policies have not been the powerful impetus for the hoped-for improvement in classroom practice.

6. The survey is part of the SERP project, Catalyzing Comprehension through Discussion and Debate. Publications of findings, including findings on implementation challenges, will be forthcoming in 2016.

7. With roots in the field of architecture where teaching design is commonplace, Michael O'Hare teaches a course in policy design at the Goldman School of Public Policy.

REFERENCES

American Association for the Advancement of Science (AAAS). 2014. "Historical Trends in Federal R&D." Retrieved from www.aaas .org/page/historical-trends-federal-rd#Agency.

American Recovery and Reinvestment Act (AARA). 2009. Retrieved from www2.ed.gov/policy/gen/leg/recovery/statutory/stabilization-fund.pdf.

Applebee, Arthur, Judith Langer, Martin Nystrand, and Adam Gamoran. 2003. "Discussion-Based Approaches to Developing Understanding: Classroom Instruction and Student Performance in Middle and High School English." *American Educational Research Journal* 40 (3): 685.

Bardach, Eugene. 2011. *Practical Guide for Policy Analysis: The Eightfold Path to More Effective Problem Solving.* 4th ed. Washington, DC: CQ Press.

Benson, Tracy, Michael Fullan, Robert Kegan, Claudia Madrazo, Joanne Quinn, and Peter Senge. 2012. "Lessons of Systematic Change for Success in Implementing the New Common Core Standards." A Report for the Hewlett Foundation Program on Deep Learning. July 4. www.academyforchange.org/wp-content /uploads/2012/08/CC7.4.12rl.pdf.

Berwick, Donald M. 2008. "The Science of Improvement." *JAMA* 299 (10): 1182–84.

Bettinger, Eric P., and Bridget Terry Long. 2009. "Addressing the Needs of Underprepared Students in Higher Education: Does College Remediation Work?" *Journal of Human Resources* 44 (3): 736–71.

Betts, Julian R., and Thomas Loveless, eds. 2005. *Getting Choice Right: Ensuring Equity and Efficiency in Education Policy.* Washington, DC: Brookings Institution Press.

Bowman, Barbara T., M. Suzanne Donovan, and M. Susan Burns, eds. 2000. *Eager to Learn: Educating Our Preschoolers.* Washington, DC: National Academies Press.

Bransford, John D., Ann L. Brown, and Rodney R. Cocking. 1999. *How People Learn: Brain, Mind & Experience in School.* Washington, DC: National Academy of Sciences.

Bryk, Anthony, Louis M. Gomez, Alicia Grunow, and Paul G. LeMahieu. 2015. *Learning to Improve: How America's Schools Can Get Better at Getting Better.* Cambridge, MA: Harvard Educational Publishing Group.

Bryk, Anthony, and Barbara Schneider. 2002. *Trust in Schools: A Core Resource for Improvement.* New York: Russell Sage Foundation.

Cawelti, Gordon 2006. "The Side Effects of NCLB." *Educational Leadership* 64 (3): 64.

Chubb, John E., and Terry M. Moe. 1990. *Politics, Markets, and America's Schools.* Washington, DC: Brookings Institution Press.

Coburn, Cynthia E. 2003. "Rethinking Scale: Moving beyond Numbers to Deep and Lasting Change." *Educational Researcher* 32 (6): 3–12.

d. school. 2010. bootcamp bootleg. Retrieved from http://dschool.stanford.edu/wp-content/uploads/2011/03/BootcampBootleg2010v2SLIM.pdf.

———. 2012. bootcamp bootleg. May 23. Retrieved from http://dschool.stanford.edu/wp-content/uploads/2011/03/BootcampBootleg2010v2SLIM.pdf.

Donovan, M. Suzanne. 2013. "Generating Improvement through Research and Development in Education Systems." *Science* 340 (6130): 317–19.

Donovan, M. Suzanne, and John D. Bransford. 2005. *How Students Learn: History, Mathematics, and Science in the Classroom.* Washington, DC: National Academies Press.

Donovan, M. Suzanne, John D. Bransford, and James W. Pellegrino. 1999. *How People Learn: Bridging Research and Practice.* Washington, DC: National Academies Press.

Donovan, M. Suzanne, and Christopher T. Cross. 2002. *Minority Students in Special and Gifted Education.* Washington, DC: National Academies Press.

Donovan, M. Suzanne, Catherine Snow, and Philip Daro. 2013. "The SERP Approach to Problem-Solving Research, Development, and Implementation." In Barry Fishman, William R. Penuel, Ann Allen, and Britte Cheng, eds., *Design-Based Implementation Research: Theories, Methods, and Exemplars,* 112:400–425. New York: National Society of the Study of Education Yearbook.

Donovan, M. Suzanne, Alexandra K. Wigdor, and Catherine E. Snow, eds. 2003. *Strategic Education Research Partnership: Commmittee on a Strategic Education Research Partnership.* Washington, DC: National Academies Press.

The Economist Intelligence Unit. 2014. "The Learning Curve: Education and Skills for Life." Retrieved from http://thelearningcurve.pearson.com/reports/the-learning-curve-report-2014.

Elmore, Richard. 1979. "Backward Mapping: Implementation Research and Policy Decisions." *Political Science Quarterly* 94 (4): 601–16.

Fryer, Roland G., Jr. 2010a. *Financial Incentives and Student Achievement: Evidence from Randomized Trials.* Vol. w15898. Washington, DC: National Bureau of Economic Research.

———. 2010b. "Financial Incentives and Student Achievement: Evidence from Randomized Trials." *NBER Working Paper Series,* #15898. April.

Glouberman, Sholom, and Brenda Zimmerman. 2002. *Complicated and Complex Systems: What Would Successful Reform of Medicare Look Like?* Toronto: Commission on the Future of Health Care in Canada.

Goddard, Roger D. 2001. "Collective Efficacy: A Neglected Construct in the Study of Schools and Student Achievement." *Journal of Educational Psychology* 93 (3): 467–76.

Griffith, George, and Lawrence Scharmann. 2008. "Initial impacts of No Child Left Behind on Elementary Science Education." *Journal of Elementary Science Education* 20 (3): 35–48.

Hannaway, Jane, and Nicola Woodroffe. 2003. "Chapter 1: Policy Instruments in Education." *Review of Research in Education* 27 (1): 1–24.

Hanushek, Eric A., and Alfred A. Lindseth. 2009. *Schoolhouses, Courthouses, and Statehouses: Solving the Funding-Achievement Puzzle in America's Public Schools*. Princeton, NJ: Princeton University Press.

Heckman, James J., and P. A. LaFontaine. 2010. "The American High School Graduation Rate: Trends and Levels." *Review of Economics and Statistics* 92 (2): 244–62.

Hoxby, Caroline M. 2003. "School Choice and School Productivity: Could School Choice Be a Tide That Lifts All Boats?" In Caroline M. Hoxby, ed., *The Economics of School Choice*, 287–342. Chicago: University of Chicago Press.

Kegan, Robert, and Lisa L. Lahey. 2009. *Immunity to Change: How to Overcome It and Unlock Potential in Yourself and Your Organization*. Boston, MA: Harvard Business Press.

Kirsch, Irwin, and Henry Braun, eds. 2016. *The Dynamics of Opportunity in America*. New York: Springer International.

Kurtz, Cynthia F., and David J. Snowden. 2003. "The New Dynamics of Strategy: Sense-Making in a Complex and Complicated World." *IBM Systems Journal* 42 (3): 462–83.

Langley, Gerald J., Ronald D. Moen, Kevin M. Nolan, Thomas W. Nolan, Clifford L. Norman, and Lloyd P. Provost. 2009. *The Improvement Guide: A Practical Approach to Enhancing Organizational Performance*. New York: John Wiley & Sons.

Lawrence, Joshua, and Catherine Snow. 2010. "Oral Discourse and Reading Comprehension." In M. Kamil, D. Pearson, E. Moje, P. Aflerback, and P. Mosenthal, eds., *Handbook of Reading Research*, vol. 4. London: Routledge.

Lionni, Leo. 1987. *Fish Is Fish*. New York: Random House.

McCaffery, Edward, and Joel Slemrod, eds. 2006. *Behavioral Public Finance*. New York: Russell Sage Foundation.

Murphy, P. Karen, Ian Wilkinson, Anna Soter, Meaghan Hennessey, and John Alexander. 2009. "Examining the Effects of Classroom Discussion on Students' Comprehension of Text: A Meta-Analysis." *Journal of Educational Psychology* 101 (3): 740–64.

NCEE. 2015. "Evaluation Brief: State Capacity to Support School Turnaround." May. Retrieved from http://ies.ed.gov/ncee/pubs/20154012/pdf/20154012.pdf.

Nelson, Richard R. 1977. *The Moon and the Ghetto.* New York: Norton.

———. 2011. "The Moon and the Ghetto Revisited." *Science and Public Policy* 38 (9): 681–90.

OECD. 2012. *Equity and Quality in Education: Supporting Disadvantaged Students and Schools.* Paris: OECD Publishing.

Podgursky, Michael J., and Matthew G. Springer. 2007. "Teacher Performance Pay: A Review." *Journal of Policy Analysis and Management* 26 (4): 909.

Pollack, Andrew, 1999. "Two Teams, Two Measures Equaled One Lost Spacecraft." *New York Times,* October 1. Retrieved from http://partners.nytimes.com/library/national/science/100199sci-nasa-mars.html.

Shonkoff, Jack P., and Deborah A. Phillips, eds. 2000. *From Neurons to Neighborhoods: The Science of Early Childhood Development.* Washington, DC: National Academy Press.

Simon, Herbert A. [1969] 1996. *The Sciences of the Artificial.* Cambridge, MA: MIT Press.

Star, Susan L., and James R. Griesemer. 1989. "Institutional Ecology, 'Translations,' and Boundary Objects: Amateurs and Professionals in Berkeley's Museum of Vertebrate Zoology, 1907–39." *Social Studies in Science* 19: 387–420.

Stein, Mary Kay, and Cynthia E. Coburn. 2008. "Architectures for Learning: A Comparative Analysis of Two Urban School Districts." *American Journal of Education* 114 (4): 583–626.

U.S. Department of Education, National Center for Education Statistics. 2003. *Teaching Mathematics in Seven Countries: Results from the TIMSS 1999 Video Study* (NCES 2003–013 Revised), by James Hiebert, Ronald Gallimore, Helen Garnier, Karen Bogard Givvin, Hilary Hollingsworth, Jennifer Jacobs, Angel Miu-Ying Chui, Diana Wearne, Margaret Smith, Nicole Kersting, Alfred Manaster, Ellen Tseng, Wallace Etterbeek, Carl Manaster, Patrick Gonzales, and James Stigler. Washington, DC.

Weiss, Carol 1982. "Policy Research in the Context of Diffuse Decision Making." *Journal of Higher Education* 53 (6): 619–39.

CHAPTER FIVE

Summary and Future Directions

LEE S. FRIEDMAN

The four preceding chapters in this book help us to take stock of the development and impact of the policy-analytic profession. This profession attempts to aid democratic decision making about public policies by informing decision makers about alternative policies available to them and the consequences of those alternatives in terms of broad public interest goals. The profession has been quite successful at making itself useful: it essentially did not exist before the 1960s, but roughly fifty years later there are over 400,000 employed analysts and public managers in the United States with graduate training in public policy and many thousands of additional analysts employed elsewhere throughout the world. The growth in the voluntary employment of analysts not only by governments of all types from local to national but by private sector and nonprofit agencies as well is a key indicator of the profession's effectiveness and value.

However, policy analysts are a demanding group, always wanting better evidence and placing a high value on self-improvement. Market tests of employment are good at establishing general value of the analytic inputs (that benefits are greater than costs), and they are also good at demonstrating the broad range of settings in which this occupation has value. But they fall short of direct evidence that the output itself is better and by how much—the policy improvements that the analysts work hard to achieve. A better understanding of when and how policy-analytic inputs succeed (and fail) at improving policies is important for learning how to improve the profession's effectiveness.

It is not easy to test the profession's effectiveness by the policy outcomes that follow after analytic input. The essential reason for this is because policy analysis is intended to complement democratic processes, not replace them by using expert judgments instead. Once one recognizes that there may be many good reasons for reaching a particular democratic decision, it becomes correspondingly more difficult to know if that decision is a better one because of the policy-analytic effort that took place while it was under consideration. Most democratic processes for making decisions are complex, subject to multiple sources of influence and pressure, and resist simple explanations of the results that follow from them.

The outcomes from political processes may not always seem wise, fair, informed, or effective. In some cases, the power of a special interest group may be readily apparent, but then in similar decisions, not so much. In cases where decisions are made through citizen votes, it can be notoriously difficult to predict (or understand) those votes. Political scientists cite many different possible reasons to explain why elected representatives vote the way that they do—personal ideology, issues of particular interest to them, party line, the interests of their jurisdiction, or courting favor with those who might help to finance their reelections. Sometimes political parties are disciplined and can align the votes of their members; at other times they are too divided to produce predictable results. Parties are not always interested in compromising to produce bipartisan policies. The contributions of policy analysis—ideas, knowledge, and expertise—matter to all of these processes but not necessarily in every decision, and it can be quite elusive to pin down its influence on actual outcomes. One way to think about the purpose of policy analysis is to give democratic processes every opportunity to come to wiser, fairer, more informed, and more effective decisions while always being respectful of the democratic ideals that underlie the processes.

It is important to appreciate the diversity of institutions within which policy analysis is used, and to be wary about overgeneralizing across those institutions. Policy analysis is used at all levels of government (local, state, national), and at each level it is used within the different branches (executive, legislative, and judicial). It is also used by nongovernmental agencies that may partner with governments or work closely with governments to achieve public interest purposes. There is no inherent reason the effectiveness of policy analysis should be the same across all of these diverse settings, or the same across all policy areas that may be considered in any one of these settings. The politics of the decision-making process in which policy-analytic inputs are embedded vary greatly across these different institutions, and the political power of stakeholders varies by policy area. In those institutions designed to bring together the widest diversity of political beliefs, it may well be harder for objective policy analysis to illuminate a preferred way forward. Conversely, in the institutions with relatively homogeneous political values, it may be easier for policy analysis to play a more significant role.

In my introductory chapter, I provide a selective overview of some of the research efforts to determine the effectiveness of policy analysis. Whether or not the research was of the case study type or of the type that compared policy processes that differ in terms of analytic inputs, the results include examples of both successes and failures of policy analysis. I observed that in these examples the successes seemed to come more from within the executive branch and the failures more from the legislative branch. This idea should be further examined, but it fits with the previous observation. That is, political values are generally more aligned within an executive branch, and this may allow more weight to be given to policy-analytic work. Values are more broadly dispersed within the legislative branch, and this may restrict the extent to which policy-analytic work can be useful in fostering agreements.

I also note in the introduction that one reason these studies face difficult challenges involves concern about how they assess "effectiveness." The general meaning of effectiveness is that the policy is improved compared to what it would have been absent the policy analysis. But how does one measure improvement, especially when public policies often have multiple goals (and thus the effect of analysis could be to do better on one goal but worse on another)?

One of these goals is usually economic efficiency, but even here it can be difficult to implement a standardized measure of a policy's effect on it. The technique of benefit-cost analysis is sometimes quite useful for this in comparing several alternatives. Extending this idea, the review includes a study of agricultural policies that uses an interesting comprehensive efficiency measure to assess policy performance differences both in any one country over time and across multiple countries at any point in time.[1] Perhaps such a measure can be replicated and routinely updated in assessing policies in other sectors like state utility regulations or health care policies. Since reducing inefficiencies is one objective of policy analysis, it can be very useful to have measures of them that can be compared both over time for any single jurisdiction and across jurisdictions. With such measures as outcomes, it may be possible to analyze the contributions to them of policy-analytic effort within the jurisdiction.

An additional problem of assessing effectiveness comes back to the definition of just what to measure. The early studies of noneffectivenss may have focused too simply on whether the analytic recommendations were adopted rather than influenced the decision in a constructive way. Later studies like Hird's (2005) emphasize improvements in the decision-making process brought about by policy analysis, such as greater transparency and greater use of evidence-based knowledge and sometimes greater trust among participants in the process. That is, policy analysis can add value to a process not only by improving the specific policies decided within it but also by improving the process itself. These kinds of findings are also important systematic effects of policy analysis. However, it can take considerable institutional learning from both analysts and decision makers to end up with a process that makes good use of the analytic resources.

Once one begins to think about process changes, it becomes apparent that policy analysis itself is often better understood as an ongoing aspect of an organizational or institutional process rather than simply a set of discrete documents that fully comprise the analyses. Many policy issues are considered by institutions that utilize a network of analysts, each playing a limited role at particular times during the decision making process, a role that may not require a written analysis. Policy reform is the resultant of the various interactions that the decision makers have with each other, with all of the different interest groups involved, and with the network of policy analysts—with the qualities and effects of these interactions dependent on the particulars of the institutional process. This idea captures a good part of what the other authors in this volume have to say about the impacts of policy analysis. For the processes they study, each of them identifies important obstacles that policy analysts must confront if they are to be effective. Furthermore, each of them offers insight about possible improvements to the effectiveness of the analysts.

Hird, for example, reports that there are practically no written policy analyses used by governments that resemble those envisioned and practiced in public policy schools. This is largely due to the institutional phenomena just described: policy analysis taking place as a process in which individual analysts each contribute different pieces at different stages of the process through their interactions with decision makers, interest groups, and one another. Nevertheless, Hird is clear that the analytic training to put all of the problem-solving steps together provides crucial skills, versatility, and a clear overall vision that enable analysts to function well in actual policy-making environments.

Hird also neatly identifies one area of public policy making that seems to be an exception to his general finding that there are no written comprehensive policy analyses: regulatory rule makings by federal agencies like the Food and Drug Administration, the Federal Communications Commission, and the Environmental Protection Agency. Since the Reagan administration, regulatory impact analyses (RIAs) have been required for all major new federal regulations. Before federal agencies can issue major new regulations, they must undertake an RIA to specify the expected benefits and costs of proposed regulations, identify and analyze all relevant alternatives, and justify the regulatory agency's choice. This provides a setting with unusual documentation that can allow further examination of evidence for or against the influence of policy-analytic knowledge in the decision, and which can give focus to interview questions asked of participants and other experts about these rule makings.

Hird is clear that the RIA requirement does not necessarily mean that there will be effective use of policy analysis. Other political forces, like those of an industry being regulated, may be strong enough to predetermine the outcome. Or the regulatory agency itself may have a predetermined outcome in mind, and simply provide the required RIA as "window dressing" rather than a conscientious and honest assessment of alternatives. But based on preliminary analysis by Desmarais and Hird (2014) that examines the citations used as evidence in the RIAs, characterizations of completely ineffective policy analysis seem unlikely. Hird reports that the citations are generally to high-quality evidence, and there would be little reason to go to the analytic trouble of identifying and singling out such evidence if it were not part of an honest effort to utilize it.

Of course this still does not mean that the RIA process is a highly effective one—Hird mentions several other studies of this process that point out some weaknesses of the RIAs—and it would be premature at this point to draw conclusions as this part of his study is ongoing. While Hird is studying the actual use of RIAs, it is of course always possible that they could be used to greater (or lesser) effect under a revised institutional process. Some scholars have suggested, for example, that an annual "regulatory budget" might add valuable discipline to the current federal regulatory rule-making process, and RIAs within such a framework could increase in importance.[2] Institutional reforms like this are another way of trying to improve the policy-making process and are worthy of further study.

Like Hird, Patashnik and Peck also consider policy analysis as an organizational or institutional process. Whereas Hird offers some new evidence on policy analysis in the regulatory processes, Patashnik and Peck focus on the U.S. Congress. Their novel approach to understanding legislative use of policy analysis is to treat Congress as a problem-solving organization charged with the responsibility to address particular types of problems, for example, how to address its oversight responsibility of the executive branch. They explain those aspects of policy analysis that are important components of this oversight task. The information it provides, for example, is what enables members of Congress to ask (if they wish) probing questions of the bureaucrats who testify and come well armed with deep knowledge of their agency's programs. It also may help to target the congressional effort on areas deserving of more intensive scrutiny (although this does not change political motivations for choosing other areas of scrutiny). There are, of course, many other potential uses of policy analysis in Congress, such as to aid design of new legislation.

This nuanced view of congressional responsibilities gives good focus to the next chapter, in which Patashnik and Peck ask how well Congress performs as a problem-solving institution given its assigned tasks. The general steps of problem solving are well known in policy analysis, for example, problem definition, assembly of evidence, construction of alternatives, identification of criteria, forecasting outcomes, consideration of trade-offs, deciding, and explaining. Based on original survey research of expert analysts in the Washington, DC, area, supplemented with detailed interviews, they assess how well Congress does at each of the problem-solving tasks. They recognize from the outset that congressional responsibilities push toward more effort at some of these problem-solving tasks than others. For example, a chief responsibility of Congress is to translate the diverse social demands from the members' constituencies into some vision that is shared enough to interest a majority and gives practical direction to a solution (the problem definition component); this same responsibility may work against consideration of a very broad set of solutions (the construction of alternatives component).

The results of this congressional assessment are decidedly mixed. The experts surveyed in April 2013 give Congress low marks as a problem-solving institution during the previous ten years. For example, 66 percent of the experts rated Congress as "poor" in terms of "making evidence-based decisions" and 56 percent as "poor" in terms of "defining problems logically." Congress was rated slightly higher in terms of "developing new policy options," but with 48 percent still giving it a "poor" rating. There were some exceptions to the generally low evaluation. A strong majority of the experts rated Congress as "fair" to "good" or "excellent" on some key aspects. Only 15 percent rated Congress "poor" in terms of "reflecting public opinion," only 21 percent "poor" in terms of "bringing attention to new issues," only 34 percent "poor" in terms of "achieving policy objectives at acceptable cost," and only 35 percent "poor" in terms of "reflecting ideas of policy experts."

To put this survey into some perspective, it is good to remind ourselves that it is the first one to evaluate Congress as a problem-solving entity. It was undertaken at a particular time when party divisions likely made it unusually difficult for Congress to agree on any legislation. This may or may not have a significant impact on the survey results; only additional surveys at different time periods could reveal this. Also, the survey evaluates Congress and not the contributions of policy analysts per se. It remains an open question whether Congress is a "better" problem solver because it is aided by many policy analysts, but the work of Patashnik and Peck helps us to gain a clearer understanding of what this might mean. For example, they do not interpret the poor score on "making evidence-based decisions" as due to any lack of analysts available to inform members about the evidence but rather legislative norms and practices that fail to promote public problem solving as a key congressional responsibility. They mention as problematic the number of complex omnibus bills covering diverse subjects that take up much congressional time. Other policy scholars, like Rivlin (2015), note this same weakness and suggest an institutional reform such as having Congress make two-year rather than one-year budgets. The reduced need to agree on a budget each year might ease the informational burden on members so that they have more time for additional problem-solving action.

Similarly, Donovan asks us to consider policy analysis as an institutional process. Her chapter is a powerful reminder that there often is a very long distance from the decision to adopt a particular policy to its actual implementation, particularly when the policy is federal and involves the delivery of complex local services. If policy analysis fails to consider adequately how alternatives will be implemented, then it introduces error into the projected outcomes and the rankings of alternatives. Donovan, drawing on the federal education initiatives for examples, faults the No Child Left Behind legislation for its failure to consider the capabilities of schools to achieve the legislation's goals. She argues that this is a too common weakness of policy analysis that relies heavily on a "market failure" framework, which leads quickly to a view of the problem as "poor incentives," to be remedied by "better incentives." The problem with this, in her experience with education initiatives, is that too many teachers, principals, and school districts do not know how to respond to these changed incentives, and they sometimes implement practices that result in worse educational outcomes than before the reform.

Donovan extends this criticism into constructive thoughts for process reforms. It is not simply that policy analysis too often ignores the capabilities of the local service providers but that a good solution may well involve sustained policy interactions to improve those capabilities. She makes an analogy to the architecture profession, in which the client and the architect interact through the design studio. The architect will generally know less than the client about how a future building is intended to be used, but the client is completely unaccustomed to conceptualizing new buildings. Therefore the architect involves the client in the building design from the beginning in order for both to learn from each other and end up with a building that will be an excellent fit for the client's purposes. Donovan believes that improving education and other complex services should naturally involve the same collaboration between the policy analysts and the service providers, as they discover together the replicable principles that work in practice to improve the complex services that are provided. Her recommendation is that policy-analytic training be expanded to include the science of design as one of its components, so that policy analysts will be better trained and follow better practices in working to improve complex services like education.

Policy analysis surely does matter. It is a great and worthy challenge to use the tools and techniques of policy analysis to contribute to the improvement of public policy making. The ideals that we have for the analytic tasks—obtaining and conveying in a timely manner accurate, relevant knowledge about alternative and innovative policies to further the public interest—must square with our ideals for democracy itself, so that the result is better democracy. Yet the rapid development and growth within the past fifty years of the policy-analytic profession that strives to achieve these ideals was neither predicted nor planned by anyone. It thrived and grew as employers like the U.S. federal government tried using their approach and found that such people could help to improve policy choices. The graduates of the first new public policy schools found gainful employment, and more and more graduate schools began adopting and offering this training. The spread of policy analysis across countries, to all levels and branches of governments and to private and nonprofit institutions that work with governments, is a reflection of the high value of these services.

But in an important sense, we have merely muddled through the growth and use of policy analysis. Politics is still politics, and policy analysis that does not complement the political process may go unutilized. The cases and systematic studies that have focused on the effects of policy analysis have found mixed results. Policy analysis can and should be made better. The substantive chapters in this volume have a common theme toward that end. The theme is to improve policy analysis by understanding it as part of an organizational or institutional process that embodies specific constraints and obstacles that policy analysts must recognize and confront.

Typically the processes limit what any one analyst can do, and they involve numerous analysts who may be at most loosely connected with one another. The processes vary by setting in terms of how the analysts interact with the decision makers and practitioners that they are trying to assist. Policy analysis within an executive branch will not be exactly the same as policy analysis for a legislature, as the responsibilities and tasks of each branch are not the same—and analysis will not be helpful if it does not address the tasks faced by the particular decision makers that it is intended to inform. The chapters in this volume help us to understand better the particular decision-making processes used in the settings that they study and help us to think more carefully about how policy analysis can be useful in those settings. Importantly, a common theme is that *the steps of problem solving used to teach individual analysts how to be effective are also useful as a way to understand the strengths and weaknesses of institutions as problem-solving entities and guide their assessments.*

We are only at the beginning of our knowledge about how best to make use of policy analysis in each of the many diverse places in which it is used. Some of the improvements may come from honing the analyses themselves—the work an analyst conveys to the decision makers, whether presented in writing or orally—to address the particular needs of the setting in which it is being used. Hird (2005) documented such changes when nonpartisan analysts working for state legislatures learned to focus on the information that legislators sought. Other improvements may come from adapting the setting to enable decision makers to make better use of the knowledge available through policy analysis. Examples of changes of this type could be reforms that enable better use of congressional time, as Patashnik and Peck recommend, or a type of regulatory budget that enhances use of the regulatory impact analyses studied by Hird. And still other improvements may come through advances in the science and art of policy analysis itself, for example, if design considerations as Donovan recommends become a part of the analyst's tool kit. Policy analysts as a group are exacting and demand good evidence, but they are also very practical. They will be pleased by any reform that enables them to better serve the public interest.

NOTES

1. See Anderson, Rausser, and Swinnen 2013.

2. A regulatory budget is a limit, similar to a governmental budget, on the total costs that may be imposed by the regulatory agencies on the entities subject to its regulations. For a recent review of this idea, see Rosen and Callanan 2014.

REFERENCES

Anderson, K., G. Rausser, and J. Swinnen. 2013. "Political Economy of Public Policies: Insights from Distortions to Agricultural and Food Markets." *Journal of Economic Literature* 51 (2): 423–77.

Haskins, Ron, and Greg Margolis. 2015. *Show Me the Evidence: Obama's Fight for Rigor and Results in Social Policy*. Washington, DC: Brookings Institution Press.

Hird, John A. 2005. *Power, Knowledge, and Politics: Policy Analysis in the States*. Washington, DC: Georgetown University Press.

Rivlin, Alice M. 2015. "Biennial Budgeting: A First Step toward Budget Process Reform." Testimony, U.S. House of Representatives Committee on the Budget, November 18.. Available at http://budget.house.gov/hearingschedule2015/does-biennial-budgeting-fit-in-a-rewrite-of-the-budget-process.htm.

Rosen, Jeffrey, and Brian Callanan. 2014. "The Regulatory Budget Revisited," *Administrative Law Review* 66 (4): 835–60.

INDEX

Note: *fig.* refers to figures